Storm Management

When You Don't Know What to Do, Do What You Know to Do

ILYNMW Publishing
Atlanta Georgia

Dedication

This book is dedicated to my Bride and the love of my life - Debbie.   She has been my constant companion and friend through all the storms in this life.   More times than not, she is the one who is throwing me a lifeline in the midst of a storm.   God has been so gracious to me in giving me a best friend who is by my side no matter what.

 In addition, I want to dedicate this book to my children - Hannah, David, Sarah and Jonathan. I am so proud of you guys and I love you no matter what!

Published by: ILYNMW Publishing

www.ILYNMW.com

v15.0

Our commitment – 100% of proceeds to Charity

Cover Design: Paul Beersdorf

ISBN 978-0-9983413-0-9

Books by Paul Beersdorf

Flowers on Tuesday

The 100 Most Important Words

Encouraging Your Wife

Encouraging Your Husband

Advice for Today, Tomorrow and Forever

Even Moses Needed Encouragement

Living Intentionally

Contents

Acknowledgements

I love my Beautiful Bride and how much she encourages me to write and share my thoughts and ideas. She is the love of my life and my best friend. Nothing I do would be worthwhile without her by my side.

I would also like to thank Junior Hill for preaching the message that was the inspiration for this book. He is an incredible man of God and I am thankful to have sat under his preaching many times.

Introduction

When I was in college (at **THE** University of Alabama – Roll Tide), I was a marketing major in the business school. I can still vividly remember my first marketing class under Dr. Morris Mayer (who later become my mentor). It was Marketing 101, the very basics and I was totally clueless about what marketing was all about.

I can remember two years prior to going to Alabama I was working at JC Penney and I had asked one of the district managers what I should major in at school, and he said "marketing". I had no idea what "marketing" was, but since he was my bosses, bosses, boss, it seemed like good advice to take.

So here I was in Marketing 101, and Dr. Mayer proceeds to tell us about the four P's of marketing. Little did I know these principles would be drilled into my head for the next two years!

The four P's of marketing are:

1. **Product**
2. **Price**
3. **Promotion**
4. **Place (distribution) they had to force the last "P"**

It has now been over 30 years since my first marketing class, and yet these four key principles of marketing have not changed one bit. I have found not only are they absolutely critical for introducing or maintaining a new product, they also do not stand alone. Each is critically dependent on the other.

If you want to introduce a new brand of cereal as an example here are the criteria (simplified) you would consider to make it successful in the market place:

Product – who is our target market (demographics), who is our competition, what is the opportunity and or unmet consumer need?

Price – home much should we charge for the new brands? What are the cost of goods (including delivery)? What is the price of similar competitive products?

Promotion – how will we advertise to let shoppers and consumers know about our new product? TV, Internet, Magazine, Bill Boards? How will we merchandise this new product in stores, on shelf, displays? Will we offer coupons?

Place – how will be distribute the product? Through customer warehouse, direct to consumer, through a third party?

As you can see, there is a lot to consider and this is only the tip of the iceberg.

The point being that every good marketer knows these four P's and applies them to each and every product line they manage. You have to know them and more importantly, you have to actually use them to be successful. You cannot just use one or two of them, you have to apply all four to meet your goals and objectives.

As I was doing some research for this book, I was amazed at the advice that is on the internet. The two most prevalent things that came up time and again for a person to do, when they did not know what to do:

1. Do nothing
2. Do something

Wow. Not exactly earth shattering and not very good or specific advice. I have never been a big fan of the "do nothing' crowd. I tend to be a person of action.

 I am also a person who believes in acting and thinking intentionally and therefore the "do something" is too vague to be helpful.

The inspiration for this book came from part of a sermon I heard from Junior Hill in 2007. He said something that just stuck with me and has been rolling around in my head ever since.

As Christians we will all find ourselves in situations where we are facing trials, troubles and tribulations. When we face those times what are we to do? That is the message of this book.

The steps to follow are really quite simple, and yet it is not simple at all. It is simple because when you are not in a crisis, it is easy to view this objectively and thoughtfully and it makes sense.

It is not simple, because when you are overwhelmed, nothing seems to make sense!

So, when you don't know what to do, these are the three things you should continue to do:

1. Pray
2. Participate in Fellowship
3. Praise & Worship

I call these the three P's of a storm management. Just like the four P's of marketing, these three P's of a storm management work together. You cannot separate them into individual components. They are meant to work together as a cohesive team to help you as you walk the path of trials, troubles and tribulation in your life.

I have been using these principles in my life for a while now and we have had a number of situations that have come up where we literally did not know what to do. We leaned into these principles and they have proven true, time and time again.

I have taught these same concepts to my children and I have seen them recognize that these truths really do work. My two adult children have had several times where we have had to rely on these truths and they have found out first-hand how true they are.

I hope you find these principles are as helpful in your life as they have been in mine. My prayer is that you would be blessed and encouraged by the words in this book. To God be the glory, great things He has done!

Storm Management

When You Don't Know What to Do, Do What You Know to Do

Storms

The first question we have to answer is whether or not we will have any storms in this life? The answer is actually quite easy if you have lived even a few years on this earth. Of course we will all have trouble, trials and tribulations in this life.

Some of us will have truly horrible situations and others will just have "speed bumps" that are annoying but not life altering.

I have heard it said many times that people are either:

- **In the middle of a storm**
- **Coming out of a storm**
- **Heading into a storm**

A storm is a good analogy because there are so many different types of real storms that we encounter in life. Some are swift and come out of nowhere like a sudden thunderstorm on a summer day. The day starts out clear and beautiful, but before you know it, you are surrounded by wind and rain. Some storms you can see coming from a long way off (like a hurricane). It is slow and plodding, but relentless and menacing. It might deviate from its path, and you might be able to avoid its full wrath, but inevitably destruction follows wherever the hurricane touches.

No matter the type of storm, being prepared and knowing what to do when the storm strikes can help you better navigate whatever comes your way.

If this is true about being in the middle of, coming out of or heading into a storm, then you sure do want to be prepared for the storms of life as they come at you.

I will use my life as an example of troubles I have faced:

- Sexual abuse
- Drug use in my family
- Wayward Children
- Death of close family members
- Miscarriage
- Physical Injury
- Sickness
- Abandonment
- Hunger (real hunger)
- Ridicule by my family
- Etc. etc. etc.

As I look at this list I know that there are many people who have faced much more than I have faced (or may ever face). However, I have had enough trouble in my life to know that I don't want anybody to have to repeat what I have been through!

With that said, I can honestly praise God for everything that has happened to me in the past. Because I know it has all brought me to a place where I can serve God and others through my life and testimony!

It is only through the healing power of Jesus Christ and His forgiveness, grace and mercy that I am able to write these words and forgive those who have harmed me in the past.

John 16:33

These things I have spoken to you, so that in Me you may have peace. In the world you have tribulation, but take courage; I have overcome the world."

Let's quickly consider two bible characters who ran into trouble (not of their own making).

- # Joseph
- # Paul

Joseph in the Old Testament

One of my favorite bible characters is Joseph of the Old Testament.   He went through some really tough times

Without retelling his entire store in detail, here is brief chronology of what happened early in Joseph's life: (told in Genesis 37-50)

- He is favored by his father (he was the youngest son at that time)
- His brothers hated him and conspired to kill him - not a good start
- Instead of killing Joseph his brothers sold him into slavery - he is 17 years old.
- He becomes a slave in Potiphar's house in Egypt
- Things go from bad to worse as Potiphar's wife falsely accuses him of molesting her
- Joseph is thrown in jail
- Joseph helps the chief cupbearer by interpreting a dream and asks for his help to get out of jail, but two years pass before he is remembered.

However, God is good and gracious to Joseph through all of this turmoil. Note that twice in Genesis 39 the bible tells us that "The Lord was with Joseph".

Joseph was 17 when he entered slavery and prison and did not get out of this situation until he was 30 years old! He spent 13 years in this situation.

So Joseph has all kinds of troubles for 13 years and it was not his fault! Finally, he is brought before Pharaoh to interpret a dream and he does something amazing.   He tells Pharaoh that he cannot interpret the dream, but that his God can interpret the dream.   This is important to note, because Pharaoh was thought to be a god himself.

This is the key turning point in Josephs life and he go on to become second in command of the country of Egypt.

God has a new plan and the next years are a different story for Joseph:

- Pharaoh (the most powerful man in the world), makes Joseph second in command. He is now running the entire country
- Pharaoh gives him a new name - Zaphenath-Paneah
- Pharaoh gives him the daughter of a high official to marry
- No one in the kingdom is greater than him other than Pharaoh
- He has two sons – and he gives them great names! **Manasseh** – which means *making to forget* and **Ephraim** – which means *fruitfulness*

Genesis 41:51-52

Joseph named the firstborn Manasseh, "For," he said, "God has made me forget all my trouble and all my father's household." He named the second Ephraim, "For," he said, "God has made me fruitful in the land of my affliction."

Clearly Joseph has gotten past his past and is in a mature enough position to praise and glorify god.

Finally, in Genesis chapter 45, Joseph confronts his brothers (who had sold him into slavery) and showers them with mercy and grace. Not only does he forgive them, but he is going to provide for their needs and the needs of their family

His bothers deserved death and instead were given life!   And not only life, but an abundant life in this time of this great famine.

Now what is great is the story of Joseph just gets better!

Another 17 year pass and now Joseph is 54 years old.   His beloved father has just passed away and his brothers fear for their lives.   They felt that the only reason they were still alive was because of their father and his relationship with Joseph.

They threw themselves at Josephs feet and said "we are your slaves"

What Joseph does next is incredible!

<u>**Genesis 50:19-21**</u>

But Joseph said to them, "Do not be afraid, for am I in God's place? As for you, you meant evil against me, but God meant it for good in order to bring about this present result, to preserve many people alive. So therefore, do not be afraid; I will provide for you and your little ones." So he comforted them and spoke kindly to them.

What you meant for evil, God meant for good! Wow, what a powerful story and unbelievable maturity to see how God worked things out and being able to give Him the praise and forgive his brothers. What a great example for us follow.

What about Paul?

Did he have any trouble or suffering?

In 2 Corinthians 11:16-33 Paul list some of his troubles:

- Stoned
- Beaten with rods three times
- Bitten by a snake
- Whipped with 39 lashes five times
- Attacked by an angry mob
- Many death threats
- Shipwrecked three times and in the ocean for a day and a night
- Criticized by other Christians
- Under arrest for two years without a trial

And on top of all of all of this he also had a "thorn in the flesh". We are never told what this was, but it obviously debilitating. How did Paul react to all of these troubles?

He chose to be content in his weakness and suffering and gain his strengths from his trust in Christ. He goes on to say in Philippians 4 that he has learned to be content no matter what his circumstance because his strength comes from Christ.

2 Corinthians 12:7-10

Because of the surpassing greatness of the revelations, for this reason, to keep me from exalting myself, there was given me a thorn in the flesh, a messenger of Satan to torment me — to keep me from exalting myself! Concerning this I implored the Lord three times that it might leave me. And He has said to me, "My grace is sufficient for you, for power is perfected in weakness." Most gladly, therefore, I will rather boast about my weaknesses, so that the power of Christ may dwell in me. Therefore I am well content with weaknesses, with insults, with distresses, with persecutions, with difficulties, for Christ's sake; for when I am weak, then I am strong.

Philippians 4:11-13

Not that I speak from want, for I have learned to be content in whatever circumstances I am. I know how to get along with humble means, and I also know how to live in prosperity; in any and every circumstance I have learned the secret of being filled and going hungry, both of having abundance and suffering need. I can do all things through Him who strengthens me.

What Paul learned was that in his own strength he could not endure, but trusting in the Lord was his strength.

Here we have two key characters in the bible who were put through the wringer of life and came out on the other side praising God. Most of us will never face what these men faced. Yet they endured, they prayed, they worshiped and they continued to fellowship with others and they gave of themselves to their family, friends and fellow believers.

So Why Are There Storms in Our Life?

To be clear there has been a ton of books, articles and sermons on this subject and I will barely scratch the surface of this topic as I want to get into the "meat" of this book.   However, I don't want you as the reader to think that I take this subject lightly or that I don't recognize that there is much deeper thought, study, reflection and mediation needed to better understand this topic.   I would highly recommend you research this subject yourself both in the bible and with other Christian commentary and literature. I will offer some brief thoughts and overview, but this is an inexhaustible subject that will be discussed for ages, with few satisfactory answers for those without faith and trust in Christ Jesus as their personal Lord and savior.

What are some of the most difficult trials we will face in our life time?

- Death of a loved one (even a spouse or child)
- Loss of employment
- Financial difficulty
- Bodily injury
- Sickness and disease
- Cancer
- Dementia or Alzheimer's

You see, the trials of life can come at us physically, mentally or financially. Sometimes it can be all three at the same time.   But I will ask these questions:

Q. Is God still God? - **YES**

Q. Can we see end to end? - **NO**

Q. Do we know his will, or his purpose in **ALL** things? - **NO**

So what do we have? What do we know?

We have FAITH! We know His word (the bible) and we have examples of those who have walked this path (faithfully) before us.

I would suggest that we spend too much time dealing with the "why". Why me? Why us? Why now? or just plain Why?

You will never be satisfied asking these questions, because they are the wrong questions. As you read through this book, I hope that you will come to realize that during these trials and tribulations, you will have choices to make and being prepared will help you both attitudinally as well as spiritually.

There is a new song on the radio right now by Hillary Scott (Grammy award winner from the group Lady Antebellum) and it is called "Thy Will Be Done". It is her first solo song that she has written and performed as a song of praise and worship to God in the midst of great tragedy in her life.

She had a miscarriage with her second pregnancy and in those moments of depths and despair she realized that God has a greater plan for her life and in writing this song she has been able to minister and touch so many people in a positive way. There is one part of the song that is very touching:- she is speaking of God and His character:

> *"I know you are good,*
> *But this does not feel good right now"*

I think that is a raw acknowledgment of the real pain we feel in those terrible moments, but then leaning back on the promises and character of God and recognizing that He is God and we are not. Thus she is able to say:

> *"Thy Will Be Done!"*

The song is so incredibly powerful and moving and God has used this song in my own life to deal with some of the trials that I am encountering. I encourage you to listen to this song, watch the videos and read the words so they can sink in and speak to your life as well.

Imagine a world without any wind – what would that be like? Completely calm lakes, seas and oceans, no messed up hair, no leaves blowing, no trees swaying and no kites flying. Also no hurricanes, thunderstorms or tornados.

Would you expect trees to fall over in this safe type of environment? Of course not. But that is exactly what happened at Biosphere 2 in the Arizona dessert.

Biosphere 2 is an enclosed environment of 3.14 acres run by the University of Arizona. In this perfect environment they planted trees that grew faster than normal and literally collapsed under their own weight.

The researches were mystified, until they discovered the lack of stress from the wind caused the trees to be weak.

You see, when the trees are put under the stress of the wind, they develop a different kind of wood call "stress wood", without getting technical, it has a different structure that allows the tree to grow stronger and better able to use the resources it needs the most (sunlight and water).

It is the stress of the wind that allows a tree to reach its full potential and literally achieve the heights it was destined for.

Consider the case of the butterfly. A young boy finds a caterpillar, puts it in a jar and brings it home. He feeds it and takes care of it, until one day it weaves a cocoon and disappears. The boy is worried, but his mother tells him the caterpillar will become a butterfly thru the process of metamorphosis.

The boy watches the cocoon for days and weeks and nothing happens, until one day, he sees it starting to move. Spell bound, he watches as the tiniest of holes appears and the butterfly struggles to emerge. Hour after hour passes and the boy becomes more anxious. He sees the struggling butterfly and feels sorry for it and wants to help.

Finally, he can wait no longer and gently cuts a bigger hole to help the butterfly escape. It finally come forth and the young boy waits for it to fly – and nothing happens! It limps around and crawls but is never able to fly or reach its full potential.

His mother reaches out to a scientist at the local college and he explains it is the very struggle to escape from the cocoon that strengths the butterfly's wings. It is only after a considerable struggle that the butterfly can ultimately free itself and in that struggle its wings become strong enough to give it flight.

If we try to avoid all the stress of life we may not reach our full potential!

The Making of a Sword

I have done some research on what it takes to make a high quality Katana samurai sword and the process is quite impressive.

It begins with the choice of steel that will be used by the master craftsman.

He is careful to only choose metal that he knows can stand the fires of the kiln, the pounding of the hammers, the raw teeth of the file, and the time consuming polishing and sanding.

It takes months and months for the master craftsman to shape and form the steel into just the right shape and configuration.

The steel first has to be heated in the fire until it is hot enough to be shaped. Then the steel is beaten with hammers until all of the impurities are removed. Time and again in the process, the steel is heated and then shaped until it finally has the desired look and feel that the master craftsman is looking for.

He will then take weeks to put a fine polish on the dull blade and sharpen it to a razors edge. He will make a custom handle that perfectly fits the hands of the new owner and a sheath to protect the final product from the elements. It will be perfectly balanced and without any imperfection.

In the end, the sword is of such high quality and durability that it will literally last for centuries and serve the owner and his family for generations. Honorably passed on from father to son.

This is what we find in Romans and James in regards to the trials and tribulations in our lives:

Romans 5:3-5

And not only this, but we also exult in our tribulations, knowing that tribulation brings about perseverance; and perseverance, proven character; and proven character, hope; and hope does not disappoint, because the love of God has been poured out within our hearts through the Holy Spirit who was given to us.

James 1:2-4

Consider it all joy, my brethren, when you encounter various trials, knowing that the testing of your faith produces endurance. And let endurance have its perfect result, so that you may be perfect and complete, lacking in nothing.

James 1:12

Blessed is a man who perseveres under trial; for once he has been approved, he will receive the crown of life which the Lord has promised to those who love Him.

What Paul and James are telling us is that it is not "if" we will face trials and tribulations, we **WILL** face trials and tribulations. There is an ultimate purpose to these trials and tribulations and it is to produce character.

Much like the making of a Katana samurai sword, it is the fires and shaping of these trials that mold us into the person God wants to be so we can be an effective instrument for His use.

God does not want us to be "dull", he wants us to be "sharp" for Him so that we can be used to further His kingdom work.

We should also consider that many times the trials and tribulations we go through are not only for our own edification and growing, but they are for encouraging and building others up in the faith as they face similar obstacles. He wants to develop our character and quality so that we can pass on these lessons and learnings to the next generation

2 Corinthians 1:3-4

Blessed be the God and Father of our Lord Jesus Christ, the Father of mercies and God of all comfort, who comforts us in all our affliction so that we will be able to comfort those who are in any affliction with the comfort with which we ourselves are comforted by God.

In my life, I have been able to use the various trials as a platform to speak into men's lives and help them come to a place of healing, forgiveness and understanding. While I would never want anyone to go through what I went through, I will praise God for my life and the work He had done (and continues to do) to mold me and make me into an instrument He can use to bring honor and glory to Him.

The trials and tribulations I am generally talking about here are not ones that we have brought on by ourselves because of foolish decisions or choices we have made.   Clearly if we have made poor choices we very well may be reaping what we have sewn.

If I was to go out and borrow money to buy a car, boat and RV (that stretches me to my financial limits) and then I suddenly lose my job or have some other financial crisis in my life, I have clearly been the one to put myself in an untenable situation and must now deal with the adverse consequences.

In the same way, if I am drinking and driving or texting and driving and cause an accident, then there will probably be very severe repercussions! There are consequences for our actions and we will be held accountable when we make poor choices or decisions.

I will be the first to tell you that I do not understand all of the how's or why's of Gods working in my life.   God did not explain himself to Job and I do not expect God to explain himself to me!

 Long ago I accepted on faith that God was my savior and creator and I put my full trust in Him.   Especially when I do not understand (that would be the very definition of faith).   To God be the glory great things he has done.

One of my favorite movies is "*RUDY*".   In one scene of the movie Rudy asks a priest about God and prayer and the priest has a pretty cool answer.

He said:

"In thirty years of study and discipleship in the church I have come up with two undeniable truths: There is a God and I am not him".

How true!!

Meaning we cannot or will not be able to explain the how's or why', but there is a God, he is in command, and he always has our best interest in mind.

Now let us consider true "storm control".

True Storm Control

When we think of storms, the biggest and baddest is the Hurricane. How powerful is a hurricane?

> ___NOAA says___ *the heat release of a hurricane is equivalent to a 10-megaton nuclear bomb exploding every 20 minutes.*
>
> ___NASA says___ *that "during its life cycle a hurricane can expend as much energy as 10,000 nuclear bombs!"*

Whether you want to believe NOAA or NASA, either way a hurricane is incredibly powerful. Tropical storm winds (39 to 73 mph) can be felt out as far as 500 miles from the eye of the storm. To put that in perspective, if the eye of the hurricane was in Atlanta, the winds would touch as far as:

Louisville Kentucky to the north
Jackson Mississippi to the west
Mrytle Beach to the east
Jacksonville Florida to the south

In other words, millions upon millions of people would be effected by a hurricane. Whether they are in the direct path or just on the periphery.

What can we do to control a storm of this size? Nothing, not a thing. We can perhaps get out of its way, but there is no guarantee of safety.

Recently Hurricane Matthew hit the eastern seaboard of the United States. This storm killed over 800 people in Haiti and Cuba and over 40 in the USA. It was a wicked powerful storm. I live in Atlanta and we had some pretty big wind gusts and some rain from the storm, even though it was hundreds of miles away. My son and I had just finished building a tree house and we watched as the trees swayed wildly and we expected the whole thing to come crashing to the ground at any minute. And there was not a thing we could do a about it!

With that said, I know ONE who can control the storm!

In Matthew, Mark and Luke each of them record the story of Jesus and how he commanded the wind and waves of a storm to stop and they did!

The disciples had spent the day with Jesus as he was doing what he did best, touching people's lives one on one and healing them.   They watched him:

- Heal a man with leprosy
- Heal Peter's mother in law
- Heal a Centurions servant

Jesus told the parable of the four soils, the parable of the mustard seed, and the parable of the seeds scattered.   He was pouring in to their lives and they watched him do miraculous things.

At the end of the day they climbed in a boat to cross the lake (the Sea of Galilee) and a violent storm arose.   Now many of the disciples were fisherman and had spent years in boats on these very waters, so they knew a real storm when they saw one.   They were literally scared to death and thought they would drown.

What was Jesus doing?   He was taking a nap! He was asleep in the middle of this tempest. He disciples woke him up and wanted to know why he did not seem to care if they died or not.

Jesus got up and told the storm "Quiet, be still" and it immediately became calm.

Jesus commands the storms, the wind the waves, and everything on heaven and earth. There is no storm to big, or care to small that Jesus does not know about it.

While we may not be able to command the storm, we stand with one who can.   He will never leave us and he will never forsake us. Into the valley of the shadow of death, He will be there with us.

When you don't know what to do, do what you know to do:

Pray
Participate in Fellowship
Praise God

Memorizing Scripture

It is important to have scripture memorized so that you can know what to reach for when you find yourself in these difficult situations.

Here are some key verses that have been helpful in my life when I am going through trials and tribulations

Psalm 119:11

Your word I have treasured in my heart that I may not sin against You.

Proverbs 3:5-6

Trust in the Lord with all your heart
And do not lean on your own understanding.
In all your ways acknowledge Him,
And He will make your paths straight.

Philippians 4:13

I can do all things through Him who strengthens me.

Romans 8:31

What then shall we say to these things? If God is for us, who is against us?

Philippians 2:13

for it is God who is at work in you, both to will and to work for His good pleasure.

Romans 8:28

And we know that God causes all things to work together for good to those who love God, to those who are called according to His purpose.

Memorizing Scripture

Matthew 11:28-30

"Come to Me, all who are weary and heavy-laden, and I will give you rest. Take My yoke upon you and learn from Me, for I am gentle and humble in heart, and you will find rest for your souls. For My yoke is easy and My burden is light."

2 Thessalonians 3:16

Now may the Lord of peace Himself continually grant you peace in every circumstance, the Lord be with you all!

Deuteronomy 31:6

Be strong and courageous, do not be afraid or tremble at them, for the Lord your God is the one who goes with you. He will not fail you or forsake you."

Romans 8:38-39

For I am convinced that neither death, nor life, nor angels, nor principalities, nor things present, nor things to come, nor powers, nor height, nor depth, nor any other created thing, will be able to separate us from the love of God, which is in Christ Jesus our Lord.

James 4:8

Draw near to God and he will draw near to you

1 John 4:4

You are from God, little children, and have overcome them; because greater is He who is in you than he who is in the world.

1 Thessalonians 5:16-18

Rejoice always;
Pray without ceasing;
In everything give thanks; for this is God's will for you in Christ Jesus.

Memorizing Scripture

Psalm 20:1

May the Lord answer you in the day of trouble!
May the name of the God of Jacob set you securely on high!

Psalm 5:11

But let all who take refuge in You be glad,
Let them ever sing for joy;
And may You shelter them,
That those who love Your name may exult in You.

Psalm 9:9

The Lord also will be a stronghold for the oppressed,
A stronghold in times of trouble;

Psalm 62:8

Trust in Him at all times, O people;
Pour out your heart before Him;
God is a refuge for us. Selah.

Psalm 27:5

For in the day of trouble He will conceal me in His tabernacle;
In the secret place of His tent He will hide me;
He will lift me up on a rock.

Isaiah 26:4

"Trust in the Lord forever,
For in God the Lord, we have an everlasting Rock.

Memorizing Scripture

Psalm 46:1

God is our refuge and strength, a very present help in trouble.

Psalm 86:7

In the day of my trouble I shall call upon You,
For You will answer me.

Psalm 18:30

As for God, His way is blameless;
The word of the Lord is tried;
He is a shield to all who take refuge in Him.

John 14:27

Peace I leave with you; My peace I give to you; not as the world gives do I give to you. Do not let your heart be troubled, nor let it be fearful.

1 Peter 5:7

Casting all your anxiety on Him, because He cares for you

When life comes up and hits you upside the head, you will not have time to run get your bible to look up that verse of wisdom or comfort. You need to hide God's word in your heart and meditate on His word daily. God's word does not return void and the deposits you make in your heart and mind will only grow dividends of peace and harmony in those deep pockets of trouble and despair.

Commit now to a regular time of bible study, mediation, memorization and prayer.

Pray

When you don't know what to do, do what you know to do.

What is that?

What are we supposed to know what to do?

As I had listed earlier in the book there are three key things you should continue to do:

- Pray
- Participate in Fellowship
- Praise and Worship God

We will start with prayer.   This seems to be the most logical starting place and this is where most people turn when they are facing adverse situations.

We will attempt to answer the following questions:

- **Why Pray?**
- **When to pray**
- **Where to pray**
- **How often?**
- **What is our posture of Prayer**

Why pray?

The best place to look for answers on prayer and the best commentary on prayer is the Bible itself.

The short answer on "why pray" is because it is effective and this is the way we communicate our wants, needs and desires to God. The Bible tells us in the book of James that the effective prayer of a righteous man can accomplish much.

I actually like how James 5:16 is rendered in different Bible translations:

James 5:16

...The effective prayer of a righteous man can accomplish much.

Depending on the translation, the verse says that prayer:

- Is Powerful
- Is Effective
- Has a mighty influence
- Can accomplish much

No matter the translation, it is clear that the intent of James was to convey to the reader that your prayers have an influence on God and that we must be persistent and bring our prayers and petitions to Him.

Let's examine the different bible verses that compel us to pray.

We will start with the book of James (a powerful and incredibly insightful book of the bible) and then follow the path of scripture as it leads us through the reasons to pray.

James 5:13

Is anyone among you suffering? Then he must pray.

This is a great start! Sometimes the easy answer is not the one we want to hear or try. We are designed for the complicated. We want some sort of high tech solution or 15 step plan. James keeps it simple - If you are suffering, pray to God!

Psalm 50:15

Call upon Me in the day of trouble;
I shall rescue you, and you will honor Me."

Psalm 91:15

"He will call upon Me, and I will answer him;
I will be with him in trouble;
I will rescue him and honor him.

Psalm 107:6

Then they cried out to the Lord in their trouble;
He delivered them out of their distresses.

Psalm 107:13

Then they cried out to the Lord in their trouble;
He saved them out of their distresses.

Psalm 81:7

"You called in trouble and I rescued you;
I answered you in the hiding place of thunder;
I proved you at the waters of Meribah.   Selah.

God is listening and wants us to bring our prayers and petitions to him. He is a good father who stands ready to rescue his children.   Note in each of the verses above the not only did God deliver them, but He also talks about being there with them in the trouble as well. Sometimes the answer does not come right away, but know that God is in your midst even in the middle of the storm.

Matthew 7:7

"Ask, and it will be given to you; seek, and you will find; knock, and it will be opened to you.

Matthew 21:22

And all things you ask in prayer, believing, you will receive."

Psalm 107:28-30

Then they cried to the Lord in their trouble,
And He brought them out of their distresses.
He caused the storm to be still,
So that the waves of the sea were hushed.
Then they were glad because they were quiet,
So He guided them to their desired haven.

Mark 11:24

Therefore I say to you, all things for which you pray and ask, believe that you have received them, and they will be granted you.

John 14:13-14

Whatever you ask in My name, that will I do, so that the Father may be glorified in the Son. If you ask Me anything in My name, I will do it.

Psalm 116:1-2

I love the Lord, because He hears
My voice and my supplications.
Because He has inclined His ear to me,
Therefore I shall call upon Him as long as I live.

Philippians 4:6

Be anxious for nothing, but in everything by prayer and supplication with thanksgiving let your requests be made known to God.

Wow – easier said than done.   How often do we worry and fret over things that have not even happened yet.   I have heard it said that 90% of the things we worry about never come to pass.

So, from all of these verses, what can we determine about prayer?

- **God is listening! He hears us!**

- **If you are suffering you should pray**

- **Call upon God when you are in trouble**

- **God will answer us when we pray**

- **God is with us all the time**

- **God wants to rescue us and save us**

- **God is with you in the storm**

I think it is important to interject here that an answer to prayer can be NO! We tend to only think in terms of God saying YES to our prayers but we must remember that only HE can see end to end and there will be times when the answer to our prayers will be no. It is at this point that we have to have the spiritual maturity to understand that there may still be things for us to learn from the troubles we are in.   God desire is to draw near to us and have us draw near to him.

Now, Let us first examine some of the different bible characters and see what we can learn about prayer in times of difficulty and adversity.

Elijah

In 1 Kings Chapter 17 & 18, we find the story of Elijah and his need for an answered prayer in his time of trouble and turmoil.

Elijah is an interesting character. He comes on the scene at a time when there were wicked kings leading that nation of Israel. He has a tough task as God is going to have Elijah confront the king and others.

How would you like to be surrounded by 850 people who did not like you? And oh by the way the King and Queen don't really care for you either!

Don't you think that perhaps praying to God would be a good thing?

Elijah was defiantly not liked or appreciated by King Ahab. Elijah was the chosen prophet of the time and he had said to King Ahab that there would be no more rain until he spoke again. Several years pass, and then Elijah goes back before King Ahab and the King is less than pleased to see him.

He calls him a "troubler, troublemaker, or destroyer of Israel". You can only imagine that this is not a good place to be in terms of your relationship with the King. The King literally had the power of life and death in his hands and being on his bad side would not bode well for you!

Elijah then goes on to challenge King Ahab and the prophets of Baal. He basically threw down the gauntlet and told the King to bring the 450 prophets of Baal and the 400 prophets of Asherah to Mount Carmel and see who served the real God.

This was life and death! If God does not answer his prayer, he will be toast!

The challenge is simple in that each group would ask God to answer with fire from heaven to take up their sacrifice.

After the prophets of Baal had failed (after Elisha has taunted them, it is really quite funny), it was Elisha's turn and this was his prayer:

At the time of the offering of the evening sacrifice, Elijah the prophet came near and said, "O Lord, the God of Abraham, Isaac and Israel, today let it be known that You are God in Israel and that I am Your servant and I have done all these things at Your word. Answer me, O Lord, answer me, that this people may know that You, O Lord, are God, and that You have turned their heart back again."

The good news is that God did answer his prayers and delivered him an incredible miracle in the face of his enemies. Read the story for yourself and be inspired by the prayer of this man of God.

Jehoshaphat

In 2 Chronicles chapter 20, we find the story of Jehoshaphat

Jehoshaphat is now King of Israel and he is suddenly faced with a huge problem. Several of his enemies have combined forces and they are going to attack. This is a life and death situation where thousands could be slaughtered. So what does Jehoshaphat decide to do?

He chooses to pray!

He acknowledges the following in his prayer to God: (verses 6-12)

- God is sovereign
- He is THE GOD
- God has the power to answer prayer
- Reminds God of His promises
- Accepts that fact that they are powerless in the face of the enemy
- He does not know what to do!

In verse 12 we see how he concludes his prayer

2 Chronicles 20:12

O our God, will You not judge them? For we are powerless before this great multitude who are coming against us; nor do we know what to do, but our eyes are on You."

Jehoshaphat knows they cannot defeat the enemy without God's assistance.

Again, God answers the prayer in a very cool way! He speaks through one of the Levites named Jahaziel and tells them the following:

- The battle belongs to God
- Do not fear
- The Lord is with them

The enemies are defeated the people of Israel did not even have to fight. God made the enemies turn on themselves and destroy each other. All that the people of Israel did was sing praises and give thanks to God as all of this unfolded before their very eyes.

I think that the three things listed above really encapsulate our relationship with God. He is with us, He does not want us to fear and He stands ready to fight the battles for us. He really is a good father. What good father does not want to do all of those things for his children?

Jonah

Many of you know the story of Jonah. He was called by God to go preach the people of Nineveh. Instead, he tries to flee from God (which is quite funny to think that there is any place we could actually hide from God) by taking a ship the farthest point from and in the opposite direction of Nineveh.

God had other plans and he is tossed from the ship after it is caught in a storm and his fellow passengers realize he is the reason for all of their troubles.

Jonah was swallowed by a great fish and was in the belly for three days and nights. While was in the stomach of the fish, he offered up prayer to God. As you can imagine, this would be a good time to pray! In Jonah chapter 2 you can read how he cried out to God and praised Him even in the midst of his unique situation.

Few of us will ever be in a predicament as challenging as Jonah, but it is clear that he was in a place where he could do nothing for himself. He was literally stuck until God was going to deliver him. He did the one thing that he knew he could do and that was to pray.

Hopefully, it is now abundantly clear that when we don't know what to do, the first thing we should do is pray and reach out to God.

I love the psalms because I can see myself in the same place as these writers. It brings me great comfort to know that others have gone before me and cried out to God and God answered them.

David

David is a character who was constantly praying to God as he faced trials and tribulations in his life (many from men trying to kill him)

- Goliath
- Saul chasing him and trying to kill him
- Absalom (his son)

You can read the many different Psalms that David wrote when he was in trouble. Here are two in particular that resonated with me as I was writing this chapter

Psalm 3: (As David is fleeing from his son Absalom)

O Lord, how my adversaries have increased!
Many are rising up against me.
Many are saying of my soul,
"There is no deliverance for him in God." Selah.
But You, O Lord, are a shield about me,
My glory, and the One who lifts my head.
I was crying to the Lord with my voice,
And He answered me from His holy mountain. Selah.
I lay down and slept;
I awoke, for the Lord sustains me.
I will not be afraid of ten thousands of people
Who have set themselves against me round about.
Arise, O Lord; save me, O my God!

For You have smitten all my enemies on the cheek;
You have shattered the teeth of the wicked.
Salvation belongs to the Lord;
Your blessing be upon Your people! Selah.

Psalm 57: (As David flees from King Saul and is living in a cave)

Be gracious to me, O God, be gracious to me,
For my soul takes refuge in You;
And in the shadow of Your wings I will take refuge
Until destruction passes by.
I will cry to God Most High,
To God who accomplishes all things for me.
He will send from heaven and save me;
He reproaches him who tramples upon me.   Selah.
God will send forth His lovingkindness and His truth.
My soul is among lions;
I must lie among those who breathe forth fire,
Even the sons of men, whose teeth are spears and arrows
And their tongue a sharp sword.
Be exalted above the heavens, O God;
Let Your glory be above all the earth.
They have prepared a net for my steps;
My soul is bowed down;
They dug a pit before me;
They themselves have fallen into the midst of it. Selah.
My heart is steadfast, O God, my heart is steadfast;
I will sing, yes, I will sing praises!
Awake, my glory!
Awake, harp and lyre!
I will awaken the dawn.
I will give thanks to You, O Lord, among the peoples;
I will sing praises to You among the nations.
For Your lovingkindness is great to the heavens
And Your truth to the clouds.
Be exalted above the heavens, O God;
Let Your glory be above all the earth.

David wrote so many of the psalms and was constantly crying out to God.
Remember that David was a man after God's own heart and he prayed
with the hope and knowledge that God was listening and would answer
his cries and petitions.   We can learn a lot by reading the psalms about
how to pray and reach out to God and the example that David gave us

The Psalms

There are so many great psalms to consider when you are in times of trouble and distress. In all of the verses below see how the Psalmist cried out in times of trouble

The psalmist used phrases like the following to describe their situation. Can you relate to any of these?

- **In the day of my trouble**
- **I will cry aloud**
- **From my Distress**
- **For I am lonely and afflicted.**
- **let my cry for help**
- **For I am afflicted and needy**
- **when I cry to You for help**

These were not people who were just a suffering a little, these were folks who were suffering a lot! They were literally crying out to God and bringing their prayers and supplications, wants and needs to the mighty God of our universe. As you read the verses that follow, know that we have a gracious heavenly father who hears our prayers and knows our needs. Know that you are not alone and that others have gone before you.

<u>Psalm 120:1</u>

In my trouble I cried to the Lord,…

<u>Psalm 107:6</u>

Then they cried out to the Lord in their trouble;….
<u>Psalm 77:1-2</u>

My voice rises to God, and I will cry aloud;
My voice rises to God, and He will hear me.
In the day of my trouble I sought the Lord;
In the night my hand was stretched out without weariness;
My soul refused to be comforted.

Psalm 118:5

From my distress I called upon the Lord;....

Psalm 25:16-17

Turn to me and be gracious to me,
For I am lonely and afflicted.
The troubles of my heart are enlarged;
Bring me out of my distresses.

Psalm 102:1-2

Hear my prayer, O Lord!
And let my cry for help come to You.
Do not hide Your face from me in the day of my distress;
Incline Your ear to me;
In the day when I call answer me quickly.

Psalm 86:1

Incline Your ear, O Lord, and answer me;
For I am afflicted and needy.

Psalm 61:1

Hear my cry, O God;
Give heed to my prayer.

Psalm 55:1

Give ear to my prayer, O God;
And do not hide Yourself from my supplication.

Psalm 70:5

But I am afflicted and needy;
Hasten to me, O God!
You are my help and my deliverer;
O Lord, do not delay.

Psalm 28:2

Hear the voice of my supplications when I cry to You for help,
When I lift up my hands toward Your holy sanctuary.

Psalm 86:6-7

Give ear, O Lord, to my prayer;
And give heed to the voice of my supplications!
In the day of my trouble I shall call upon You,
For You will answer me.

Psalm 142:1-2

I cry aloud with my voice to the Lord;
I make supplication with my voice to the Lord.
I pour out my complaint before Him;
I declare my trouble before Him.

Before I wrote this book, I was not a great student of the Psalms.   I always spent most of my time in Proverbs on a daily basis. However, I have come to realize how powerful and beautiful the psalms are and how they speak to my heart, mind, body and soul.

I pray you will take the time to become a student of the psalms and not just a reader of the psalms.

Now that we have seen how the Psalmist cried out to God, let see how God answered those prayers.

How God Answers Those Who Pray

Now let's see how God answered when people cried out to Him:

God is always listening! He never sleeps, he never slumbers, and He is good father who only wants the best for his children.   His ears are open and his eyes are constantly seeking.

Psalm 50:15

Call upon Me in the day of trouble; I shall rescue you, and you will honor Me."

Psalm 3:4

And He answered me from His holy mountain.   Selah.

Psalm 118:5

The Lord answered me and set me in a large place.

Psalm 107:6

He delivered them out of their distresses.

Psalm 138:3

On the day I called, You answered me; You made me bold with strength in my soul.

Psalm 120:1

In my trouble I cried to the Lord, And He answered me.

Psalm 34:4

I sought the Lord, and He answered me,And delivered me from all my fears.

Psalm 28:6

Blessed be the Lord,
Because He has heard the voice of my supplication.

Psalm 145:18-19

The Lord is near to all who call upon Him,
To all who call upon Him in truth.
He will fulfill the desire of those who fear Him;
He will also hear their cry and will save them.

Psalm 34:15

The eyes of the Lord are toward the righteous
And His ears are open to their cry.

So in all of the verses from Psalms where we see God answering. What were the answers?

- **Deliverance and rescue**
- **Set in a large place**
- **Fulfilled desire**
- **Boldness**
- **Strength**

These are exactly the things we need when we call out to God in our distress and times of trouble.

We can now example the following questions

Q. When is the right time to pray?

Q. Where is the right place to pray?

Q. Our posture during prayer?

When to Pray

So when should we pray? Is there one time of day that is better than another? Is there a day of the week or month of the year that will be better for us to offer our prayers to God? Of course not! God is constantly there to hear our prayers and petitions.

- **Pray in the morning** – Psalm 5:3, Mark 1:35, Psalm 88:13
- **Pray at noon** – Acts 10:9
- **Pray all night** – Acts 16:25, Luke 6:12, Psalm119:62
- **Pray several times per day** – Daniel 6:10
- **Pray without ceasing** – 1 Thessalonians 5:17, Psalm 119:64

Where to Pray

- **In secret** – Matthew 6:6
- **Riverside** – Acts 16:1
- **Mountain Top**- Luke 6:12, Mark 6:46
- **Secluded place** – Mark 1:35
- **Roof** – Acts 10:9
- **Wilderness** – Luke 5:16
- **Everywhere** – 1 Timothy 2:8

Posture of Prayer

- **Sitting** – 2 Samuel 7:18, Judges 20:26
- **Lifting Hands** – 1 Timothy 2:8
- **Face Down** – Numbers 20:6
- **Looking Up** – John 17:1
- **Lying Down** - Psalm 63:6
- **Prostrate** – Matthew 26:39
- **Bow Down** – Psalm 95:6
- **Kneeling** - Daniel 6:10, Luke 22:41, 2 Chronicles 6:13
- **Standing** - 2 Chronicles 20:5-6, 2 Chronicles 20:13, Genesis 24:12-14, 1 Samuel 1:26, 1 Kings 8:22, Mark 11:25

Prayer Recap

Let me recap the fundaments of prayer that you have been reading about in this chapter:

1. Why Pray – because it is effective and God is listening

2. When should we pray – all the time!

3. What should our posture be when we pray? It does not matter! God can hear your prayers no matter the position of you body.

You see, too many people make prayer much too complicated.   It is not complicated at all! God can hear you prayer:

From the highest mountain,
To the deepest sea,
From the belly of a fish,
To a jail cell at midnight,
From the middle of a storm,
To the quiet of an olive orchard at night,
In the face of a blazing furnace,
Or in the face of those with stones in their hands,
From a lions den,
Or before a giant in the land,
From a cave when you are being pursed,
To the temple before the people,
Eyes open,
Eyes closed,
Hands held high,
Head bowed down,
Sitting up,
Laying down,
Morning, noon and night
Rain or Shine
24/7/365

You just have to reach out to God! Draw near to God and he will draw near to you.

James 4:8
Draw near to God and He will draw near to you

Prayer Quotes

"Prayer is a shield to the soul, a sacrifice to God, and a scourge for Satan". John Bunyan

"More things are wrought by prayer than this world dreams of." Alfred Lord Tennyson

"The fewer the words the better prayer." Martin Luther

"Prayer does not fit us for the greater work; prayer is the greater work." Oswald Chambers

"Prayer is an effort of will." Oswald Chambers

"Pray as if everything depended on God, and work as if everything depended upon man." Francis J. Spellman

"God does nothing but by prayer, and everything with it." John Wesley

"Our prayer and God's mercy are like two buckets in a well; while one ascends, the other descends." Arthur Hopkins

"It is because of the hasty and superficial conversation with God that the sense of sin is so weak and that no motives have power to help you to hate and flee from sin as you should." A.W. Tozer

"Prayer is not monologue, but dialogue. Gods voice in response to mine is its most essential part". Andrew Murray

"Every great movement of God can be traced to a kneeling figure." D. L. Moody

"Don't pray when you feel like it. Have an appointment with the Lord and keep it. A man is powerful on his knees." Corrie Ten Boom

Prayer Quotes

"Work as if you were to live a hundred years. Pray as if you were to die tomorrow." Benjamin Franklin

"Prayer is the acid test of devotion." ~ Samuel Chadwick

"Prayer requires more of the heart than the tongue."
Adam Clarke

"Prayer – secret, fervent, believing prayer – lies at the root of all personal godliness.+ Williams Carey

Participate In Fellowship

What is the importance of fellowship in the middle of a storm? In times of trial, trouble and tribulation?

It is about giving and receiving encouragement!

Sometimes when we are having troubles in our life we may not want to be in the presence of others. It is easier to hide in our homes, and not let others see that we are hurting and wounded. It is easy to hide our feeling and our sorrows when we are not around anyone else. Also it might actually be embarrassment or pride that keeps us from fellowship with others as well.

But that is actually the last thing we need to do! We need to continue in fellowship so that we can be encouraged by others.

In the early church the members came together to fellowship and worship and encourage on another. No doubt there was persecution and trials for these earlier believers, but they knew that there was strength in their numbers and they could lean upon and trust one another to get through each day. We can see this in Acts chapter two as the new believers came together to encourage one another.

Acts 2:41-47

So then, those who had received his word were baptized; and that day there were added about three thousand souls. They were continually devoting themselves to the apostles' teaching and to fellowship, to the breaking of bread and to prayer.

Everyone kept feeling a sense of awe; and many wonders and signs were taking place through the apostles. And all those who had believed were together and had all things in common; and they began selling their property and possessions and were sharing them with all, as anyone might have need.

Day by day continuing with one mind in the temple, and breaking bread from house to house, they were taking their meals together with gladness and sincerity of heart, praising God and having favor with all the people. And the Lord was adding to their number day by day those who were being saved.

The book of Hebrews was written to Jewish believers who had come to know and trust Christ as their personal Lord and Savior. They would have been shunned by their families and perhaps persecuted by the Roman authorities and yet through all this the writer (many believe to be Paul) tells the believers that it is important for them to continue in fellowship.

Hebrews 10:24-25

and let us consider how to stimulate one another to love and good deeds, not forsaking our own assembling together, as is the habit of some, but encouraging one another; and all the more as you see the day drawing near.

This is the example we want to follow. It is not only the love we will receive in words and hugs, but also the good deeds (which can be as simple as a meal or flowers) or could be actual deeds of service to help others (driving a loved one to the store, or doctor visit, helping get kids to school or sports event). Encouragement can take many different forms and shapes to meet the needs of others.

Romans 15:4-6

For whatever was written in earlier times was written for our instruction, so that through perseverance and the encouragement of the Scriptures we might have hope. Now may the God who gives perseverance and encouragement grant you to be of the same mind with one another according to Christ Jesus, so that with one accord you may with one voice glorify the God and Father of our Lord Jesus Christ.

So how do we encourage one another?

1 Thessalonians 5:11

Therefore encourage one another and build up one another, just as you also are doing.

In the bible we find many examples of people who were encouraging one another and helping them in times of stress, troubles, trials, preparation and pain.   We will examine several of these relationships:

- **Ruth & Naomi – dealing with death & disappointment**
- **Arron & Moses – challenging authority**
- **Moses & Joshua – change in leadership**
- **Mary and Elizabeth – dealing with difficult situation**
- **Paul & Timothy – mentoring**
- **Jonathan & David – friends in distress**
- **Barnabas & Saul - a new believer**

Ruth & Naomi

In the book of Ruth we find that Ruth comes along side of Naomi after the death of her husband and two sons.   Ruth says the most incredible and encouraging thing to Naomi in the depths of her despair.   Naomi has just told Ruth that she can go back to her own people and to basically forget about her.

Ruth 1:16-17

But Ruth said, "Do not urge me to leave you or turn back from following you; for where you go, I will go, and where you lodge, I will lodge. Your people shall be my people, and your God, my God. Where you die, I will die, and there I will be buried. Thus may the Lord do to me, and worse, if anything but death parts you and me."

This is such a powerful statement of encouragement that many people include it in their marriage vows.

What an incredible thing for Naomi's to hear at this lowest point in her life. It would have been very easy for Ruth to take the easy way out, but she chose love and loyalty over the easy and convenient. What an unbelievably positive example for all of us!

Naomi now had a loyal companion to carry her burden, to travel with, to talk to and share fond memories. While I am sure Naomi was still in grief and sorrow, she must have also been greatly encouraged by the loyalty and love of Ruth.

Arron & Moses

Moses is one of the best know characters in the Old Testament. His exploits and deeds are known even to the casual observer of history. From his humble beginnings as an innocent baby in a basket to his rise as a leader of his people, Moses was a mighty man used by God.

As a reminder, here are a few things Moses experienced:

- God speaking from a burning bush
- Confronting Pharaoh - the most powerful man in the world
- Parting the Red Sea
- Water from a Rock
- Manna from Heaven
- Brought forth the 10 Commandments

Moses seems like a larger than life character that could not possibly be real. He seems to be super human, beyond the reach of us mortals. And yet, as you read about his life, you realize he was just a man, and as such, he needed help and encouragement just like the rest of us.

It is interesting to note that Moses was somewhat of a reluctant leader who did not want to speak before Pharaoh. He did not have the self confidence in himself and questioned his abilities. Moses doubted himself, doubts the people will listen to him and doubts anyone will believe him.

Follow this progress as God commands Moses to confront Pharaoh, who, by the way, is the most powerful man in the world at this time (this might also give you "pause" when you really think about it).

Moses is going to make several excuses to God that he hopes will keep him from having to confront Pharaoh.
Moses will pose several questions to God:

- Who am I to do this task?
- Who are you and what should I tell the people who you are?
- What if the people don't believe me?

(As a side note, I think it is somewhat amusing that Moses has these doubts and questions in the first place. Why do I think it is amusing? Because he is talking to a burning bush that is not being consumed, and this is an incredible miracle in and of itself. Yet he has all these doubts. You would think this was enough of a miracle to convince him.)

In Chapter 3 of the book of Exodus, we pick up the story:

God tells Moses to confront Pharaoh and this is Moses response:

Exodus 3:11

But Moses said to God, "Who am I, that I should go to Pharaoh, and that I should bring the sons of Israel out of Egypt?"

Remember that Moses has been away from Egypt for a really long time. He is basically just a shepherd and has been leading a simple life. How will he confront the most powerful man in the world? And more importantly, go back to a country he fled because he had murdered an Egyptian - where certain death awaits him.

God offers the first encouragement to Moses when he doubts himself and his ability to confront Pharaoh.

Exodus 3:12

And He said, "Certainly I will be with you, and this shall be the sign to you that it is I who have sent you: when you have brought the people out of Egypt, you shall worship God at this mountain."

You would think that would enough encouragement for God to say **"I will be with you".** Those are such powerful words of encouragement.

But Moses continues to make excuses. He asks God another question:

Exodus 3:13

Then Moses said to God, "Behold, I am going to the sons of Israel, and I will say to them, 'The God of your fathers has sent me to you.' Now they may say to me, 'What is His name?' What shall I say to them?"

So Moses asks this question and God gives Moses the perfect answer:

Exodus 3:14

God said to Moses, "I AM WHO I AM"; and He said, "Thus you shall say to the sons of Israel, 'I AM has sent me to you.'"

From the different commentaries I have read, what God is conveying to Moses about his character in this statement is the following:

- I AM - Self-existent
- I AM - Eternal
- I AM - Unchangeable
- I AM - Faithful and True

This should also have been incredibly encouraging to Moses to know that not only is God with him, but He is faithful and true, never changing and ever present.

God goes on to tell Moses that the elders and people of Israel will listen to him and he needs to go to Pharaoh.

However, Moses has one last excuse up his sleeve:

Exodus 4:1

Then Moses said, "What if they will not believe me or listen to what I say? For they may say, 'The Lord has not appeared to you.'"

Moses again is looking for the reassurance and encouragement before he will go on to do the task set before him. God is good and gracious to be patient with Moses and offer him the encouragement he needs.

God then give Moses the ability to perform two miracles. His staff turns into a snake and his hand become leprous when he puts it in his cloak and then is healed when he puts it back in his cloak. God is loading up Moses with everything he needs to be successful and complete his mission.

Exodus 4:2-8

The Lord said to him, "What is that in your hand?" And he said, "A staff." Then He said, "Throw it on the ground." So he threw it on the ground, and it became a serpent; and Moses fled from it. But the Lord said to Moses, "Stretch out your hand and grasp it by its tail" – so he stretched out his hand and caught it, and it became a staff in his hand – "that they may believe that the Lord, the God of their fathers, the God of Abraham, the God of Isaac, and the God of Jacob, has appeared to you."

The Lord furthermore said to him, "Now put your hand into your bosom." So he put his hand into his bosom, and when he took it out, behold, his hand was leprous like snow. Then He said, "Put your hand into your bosom again." So he put his hand into his bosom again, and when he took it out of his bosom, behold, it was restored like the rest of his flesh. "If they will not believe you or heed the witness of the first sign, they may believe the witness of the last sign.

So Moses has now seen three miracles - the burning bush, the staff to a snake and the leprous hand. As if this is not enough, God gives Moses one more "trump card". The ability to turn water into blood.

Exodus 4:9

(This is God speaking to Moses) - *But if they will not believe even these two signs or heed what you say, then you shall take some water from the Nile and pour it on the dry ground; and the water which you take from the Nile will become blood on the dry ground."*

Therefore, God has now answered all of Moses questions and encouraged him in three specific ways:

1. "I will be with you"
2. "I AM WHO I AM"

3. Gives Moses the ability to perform miracles

This is still not enough for Moses; he starts to whine about his inability to speak and wants out of his mission. God is angry but finally relents and sends Moses brother Aaron onto the scene to help.

Clearly Moses needed someone by his side to offer encouragement and help carry the load.

Aaron turns out to be an incredible companion.   God sends him into the mountains to meet Moses and there Moses tells him everything that God wants them to do.   At this point, they have formed a powerful team.

I love how God is willing to be patient and have this loving, back and forth conversation with Moses and help relieve his fears, offer encouragement and even send someone to be by his side.   We should remember this example as parents or leaders when we need others to perform a difficult task.   They may have doubts and fears and we should be patient and listen.   We should look for solution and offer encouragement and make sure we equip them with all the "tools" they will need to be successful.

Now Moses and Aaron are off to see Pharaoh.

You may have never noticed how closely Moses and Aaron are linked during this incredibly trying time as the nation of Israel tries to break free from their slavery and bondage.   Note that Aaron is right there by the side of Moses through it all.

I had never noticed before all the verses where it says "Moses and Aaron" More than 20 times do you see their names linked together.

From chapters 4-12 in the book of Exodus, almost every time you see the name of Moses you see Aaron's name as well.   No doubt this was a great encouragement to Moses.   You see, Moses was just a normal man that God chose to use in extraordinary ways.

 In the same way you and I need others to be our "Aaron" and come beside us and at other times, we need to become "Aaron" to others and be an encourager to them.   In these examples, Aaron is the mouth piece and companion for Moses.

So Moses is able to accomplish the mission set before him because God is able to adequately encourage him along the way.

In this next example you will see how Aaron was able to offer encouragement in a very different way.

In the time that Moses had lead the people out of Egypt, there was much groaning and moaning as they confronted different obstacles. God parted the Red Sea, brought them manna from heaven and water from a rock. Now they must confront an enemy in battle.

We are introduced to Joshua at this juncture of the story and Joshua is now commanded to go and fight the Amalekites Moses promised victory as long as he held the staff of God in his hands.

Here is where Aaron and Hur are able to offer physical encouragement to Moses.

Read the following verses:

Exodus 17:8-13

Then Amalek came and fought against Israel at Rephidim. So Moses said to Joshua, "Choose men for us and go out, fight against Amalek. Tomorrow I will station myself on the top of the hill with the staff of God in my hand." Joshua did as Moses told him, and fought against Amalek; and Moses, Aaron, and Hur went up to the top of the hill. So it came about when Moses held his hand up, that Israel prevailed, and when he let his hand down, Amalek prevailed. ***But Moses' hands were heavy. Then they took a stone and put it under him, and he sat on it; and Aaron and Hur supported his hands, one on one side and one on the other.*** *Thus his hands were steady until the sun set. So Joshua overwhelmed Amalek and his people with the edge of the sword.*

You see, sometimes we just need to come alongside someone and help them physically to encourage them. In this case, they were literally holding Moses hands up. Moses needed these men to come alongside him to help complete the task.

We cannot and should not expect our leaders to do all the work themselves. Leaders need help and encouragement as much as anybody else.

Try to imagine who was encouraged that day.

1. The Israelites watching the battle would have been so encouraged to see their leader on the hill overlooking the battle and Joshua in the valley fighting for them.
2. Joshua would have been encouraged to know his leaders were doing everything in their power to help him be successful
3. Moses would have been encouraged by the love and devotion of these men to help him.
4. Aaron and Hur would have been encouraged by seeing the positive impact of their intervention and help.

Encouragement pays big dividends for everyone involved. It has ripple effects that you may not even see in your life time. Later in the book you will see how Moses encourages Joshua as he takes the reins as the new leader of the nation of Israel.

Moses & Joshua

Have you ever been the one waiting in the wings for your time on the main stage? You have watched your mentor and leader for years and soon it will be your turn to be the leader. That can be very intimidating for anyone to handle. There will be doubts and fears and perhaps thoughts of inadequacy.

The leader in this case is Moses. Moses has been a great leader and God has used him in a miraculous way to lead the people of Israel out of Egypt. Moses has taken them across the Red Sea and into the wilderness for 40 years. He has been their one constant since they have left their slavery and oppression. A whole generation has grown up in the wilderness and only knows the stories of Egypt that have been passed down from their elders.

Moses is a great leader and realizes that his time has passed and God will not allow him to cross over into the Promised Land. Therefore, he wants to encourage the people before they continue their journey.

<u>Deuteronomy 31:6</u>

Be strong and courageous, do not be afraid or tremble at them, for the Lord your God is the one who goes with you. He will not fail you or forsake you."

These are powerful words that must have filled the people's hearts with hope and encouragement.

Moses gives then three distinct points that should help them to be strong and courageous. He tells the people:

1. God will go with you

2. God will not fail you (God is faithful) some translations say that God will not leave you

3. God will not forsake you

As you read these words think about others who may be heading into the "Wilderness" and how you can encourage them today. What are some "Wilderness" areas that someone may be heading into? Here are a few that give people some "pause":

- New job
- Marriage
- Birth of a child
- Loss of loved one
- Moving to a new city or country
- A physical or mental challenge

These "wilderness" areas can be scary because they are new territory that has never been tread before. However, those same words that Moses spoke to the nation of Israel are true for you today. In addition we have some additional powerful scripture to encourage us as we head into the "wilderness". Consider these two verses:

Romans 8:31

What then shall we say to these things? If God is for us, who is against us?

1 John 4:4

You are from God, little children, and have overcome them; because greater is He who is in you than he who is in the world.

These are great verses to memorize and have ready for instant recall. They have been a great comfort to me in times of trouble and distress.

PASSING THE TORCH

They say that it is lonely at the top because everyone is looking at you and you have no one to confide in and talk to. Joshua is about to find out.

All this time Joshua has been sitting in crowd watching and learning from this great leader and now it will soon be his turn to lead. Moses is not done, he knows that he must have a discussion with Joshua and pass the torch. He knows how difficult it is to be a leader and how lonely and challenging the task will be for Joshua. Moses knows this and wants to offer some personal words of encouragement to Joshua as he gets ready to take the reins.

Deuteronomy 31:7-8

*Then Moses called to Joshua and said to him in the sight of all Israel, "**Be strong and courageous,** for you shall go with this people into the land which the Lord has sworn to their fathers to give them, and you shall give it to them as an inheritance. The Lord is the one who goes ahead of you; He will be with you. He will not fail you or forsake you. Do not fear or be dismayed."*

Moses offers Joshua the same encouragement that he offered the nation of Israel:

1. God will go with you
2. God will not fail you (God is faithful) some translations say that God will not leave you
3. God will not forsake you

Like any good leader, Moses knows that you need to offer the same message over and over again so that it will sink in and people will take it to heart.

Moses has done his job and is finishing well.   He has encouraged Joshua and is now ready to let him be the new leader.

Moses passes away and now reality of leadership hits Joshua full force. He is "the man".   He must now lead.

Then God steps in and starts Joshua on his journey with some very strong encouragement.

In the next passage you will see that three times God says to Joshua:

"BE STRONG AND COURAGEOUS"

"BE STRONG AND COURAGEOUS"

"BE STRONG AND COURAGEOUS"
God knows what lies ahead for Joshua and he is preparing him for leaderships and the challenge he will face.

God then tells Joshua two key things:

1. "I will never leave you nor forsake you"
2. "... the Lord your God will be with you wherever you go"

On the first item, God is reminding Joshua what Moses had already told him earlier. Moses had used these exact same words to describe how God would treat Joshua.

On the second item, it is God's way to reminding Joshua that he will never be alone in his leadership. God was going to be with him and Joshua would need to learn how to lean into God in times of trouble and doubt.

Read the verses below and be encouraged and know that we serve a great God who is always looking for ways to encourage his children.

(note the emphasis in the passage has been added by me)

This is God speaking to Joshua:

Joshua 1:5-9

..."*No man will be able to stand before you all the days of your life. Just as I have been with Moses, I will be with you; I will not fail you or forsake you. **Be strong and courageous**, for you shall give this people possession of the land which I swore to their fathers to give them. **Only be strong and very courageous**; be careful to do according to all the law which Moses My servant commanded you; do not turn from it to the right or to the left, so that you may have success wherever you go. This book of the law shall not depart from your mouth, but you shall meditate on it day and night, so that you may be careful to do according to all that is written in it; for then you will make your way prosperous, and then you will have success. Have I not commanded you? **Be strong and courageous**! Do not tremble or be dismayed, for the Lord your God is with you wherever you go.*"

We are all leaders in one way or another. Consider these words and think about how you need to constantly be offering words of encouragement to those who are following you. By offering the same message over and over again, you will let them know you are consistent in your words and deeds and that they can trust you.

If a consistent message from God is good enough for Joshua, it is good enough for you and I today.

Mary and Elizabeth

Most scholars believe that Mary was a teenager when she became the mother of Jesus.   I don't know about you, but when I was a teenager I was not even prepared to take care of myself, much less a family.

As a father with two teenage daughters, I cannot begin to imagine what might have been going through her heart and mind as she went through this phase of her life.   I am sure her heart and mind were filled with all manner of thoughts, fears and doubts.

I do know that it would have been important for her to be encouraged during this critical time in her life.

After the angel Gabriel spoke to Mary and told her that she would be the mother of Jesus, she immediately went to see her cousin Elizabeth.

Why did she go?

- Gabriel had told her that Elizabeth was expecting a child (even in her old age)
- Mary would have wanted to have someone to talk to and confide in
- Mary knew that Elizabeth would most likely be sympathetic
- Mary would need some help in the 1st trimester as this can sometimes be very challenging.

So Mary goes to Elizabeth not knowing what to expect.   Will she be welcomed? Will she be criticized, ostracized?

What she receives is encouragement and reassurance when she sees her cousin Elizabeth.

Luke 1:39-45

Now at this time Mary arose and went in a hurry to the hill country, to a city of Judah, and entered the house of Zacharias and greeted Elizabeth. When Elizabeth heard Mary's greeting, the baby leaped in her womb; and Elizabeth was filled with the Holy Spirit. And she cried out with a loud voice and said, "Blessed are you among women, and blessed is the fruit of your womb! And how has it happened to me, that the mother of my Lord would come to me? For behold, when the sound of your greeting reached my ears, the baby leaped in my womb for joy. And blessed is she who believed that there would be a fulfillment of what had been spoken to her by the Lord."

So now Mary knows that what she heard from Gabriel is true and God has given her reassurance and encouragement through the words of her cousin Elizabeth.
She stays with Elizabeth for three months and then returns home and time passes by.

A census is now required throughout the land and she and Joseph went to Bethlehem (because that was his home town) to be counted.

While there she gave birth to Jesus and a group of shepherds came to see the baby and proclaim to all what had happened that night.

Luke 2:17-19

When they (the shepherds) *had seen this* (Mary and the Baby*), they made known the statement which had been told them about this Child. And all who heard it wondered at the things which were told them by the shepherds. But Mary treasured all these things, pondering them in her heart.*

Now not only had Mary heard from her cousin Elizabeth, but now some local shepherds had also spoken about Jesus and how special he was, that He was the Christ. It then says that Mary pondered this in her heart. I like to think that this is just another example of God reassuring a young mother and encouraging her.

A lot has been happening and eight days quickly pass since the shepherds had come to see her and Jesus in the manger. It is time to take the baby to temple to be circumcised. This is a pretty normal event in a Jewish baby's life.

However, God is going to continue to encourage and reassure Mary by having a righteous man named Simeon speak into her life.

Simeon had been reassured by the Holy Spirit that he would not die before he saw the Lord Christ. Simeon was at the temple the day when Jesus was brought to be circumcised. See what happens next:

Luke 2:27-33

And he (Simeon) came in the Spirit into the temple; and when the parents brought in the child Jesus, to carry out for Him the custom of the Law, then he took Him into his arms, and blessed God, and said,

"Now Lord, You are releasing Your bond-servant to depart in peace, According to Your word; For my eyes have seen Your salvation, Which You have prepared in the presence of all peoples, A Light of revelation to the Gentiles, And the glory of Your people Israel."

And His father and mother were amazed at the things which were being said about Him.

So, once again God uses an individual to speak into Mary's life and encourage here in regard to her baby boy.

As some more time passes, Mary is about to be encouraged and reassured by a group of Magi (wise men).

Most scholars believe that Jesus would have been 1-2 years old by the time the Magi sought him out to bring him gifts and worship him.

Matthew 2:7-11

Then Herod secretly called the magi and determined from them the exact time the star appeared. And he sent them to Bethlehem and said, "Go and search carefully for the Child; and when you have found Him, report to me, so that I too may come and worship Him." After hearing the king, they went their way; and the star, which they had seen in the east, went on before them until it came and stood over the place where the Child was. When they saw the star, they rejoiced exceedingly with great joy. After coming into the house they saw the Child with Mary His mother; and they fell to the ground and worshiped Him. Then, opening their treasures, they presented to Him gifts of gold, frankincense, and myrrh.

Mary would have been going through all the usual paces of a young mother and wife during this time; making a home, taking care of a young child and being a young bride.

In other words, she would a have been very busy just taking care of the day to day duties and not really thinking about the future. What an incredible opportunity for God to encourage and reassure her of who her son was and how special he would be.

Think about all the different people God used to encourage and reassure a young mother:

- Elizabeth her cousin - before he is born
- Shepard boys - at his birth
- Simeon - at the temple
- Magi - as a toddler

Consider who God uses to offer Mary encouragement:

- ✓ A close family member
- ✓ Poor strangers (very lowly in stature)
- ✓ A Godly/Righteous man
- ✓ Rich Wise men

In other words, she has been encouraged by the major facets of society at that time. God clearly wanted her to receive the message of encouragement for a very eclectic group of individuals, so that she would have to know it was from God.

I believe that God knew that Mary would need each of these instances to encourage her and reassure her of the words she first heard from Gabriel at the very beginning.

Jonathan & David

Who was David really?   He was the youngest son of Jesse and not even big enough to be considered worthy of doing anything other than being a shepherd.   However, God does not look at the outward appearance of David, but considers his heart and knows that he will be the next King of Israel.

God has rejected King Saul as the leader of Israel and has sent the prophet Samuel to anoint the next King.   Samuel goes to see Jesse and all of his oldest sons are brought before him and Samuel looks at them and thinks that surely one of them is "the man".   This is what God say's though:

1 Samuel 16:7

But the Lord said to Samuel, "Do not look at his appearance or at the height of his stature, because I have rejected him; for God sees not as man sees, for man looks at the outward appearance, but the Lord looks at the heart."

Therefore, David is brought from the fields and presented to Samuel. God chooses David and his is anointed by Samuel to be the next King of Israel.

God now sets David on a path to interact with King Saul.

First David is brought to the palace to soothe the King with fine music when his mind is troubled.   This then sets up one of the most famous events in the bible.

David .vs Goliath.

We all know about David and Goliath, and the great victory that David had over the Philistine giant.   Even today this story is used to describe any battle of small and weak .vs large and strong.

With one stone, David is able to encourage the entire army and they chase the Philistines army back to their own country.

While this is a famous story, fewer people have studied the relationship between David and Jonathan and know how Jonathan offered encouragement to David at a crucial time in his life.

You have to know that Jonathan is the son of King Saul and that would mean that he is next in line to be King. An appropriate title for Jonathan today would be Prince Jonathan. When his father died, he would be King of Israel. This is important to note, because it will help you to better understand how incredible it is that Jonathan becomes a key encourager in David's life.

Here is a brief set up of the events that lead to Jonathan encouraging David.

- David has slain Goliath
- Jonathan and David "become one in the spirit" and best friends
- Saul keeps David with him all the time now
- David and Jonathan become close friends
- The people praise David over King Saul for having killed more men
- King Saul becomes jealous and sets out to kill David
- King Saul pursues David to kill him

David is a young man and now fears for his life.

The KING wants him dead. Who wants to have the leader of a country as your enemy? I don't know about you, but I would be trembling with fear. Imagine making an enemy of the President of the United States and now his mission is to have you killed. He will use all of his resources at his disposal to end your life. Pretty scary stuff!

When you are in great fear of death, don't you think this would be a good time for encouragement?
Who would expect the encouragement to come from the Kings son???

He is next in line to be King and this is his father. However, Jonathan chooses loyalty to David. See how this starts to play out and note the final sentence in verse four.

1 Samuel 20:1-4

Then David fled from Naioth in Ramah, and came and said to Jonathan, "What have I done? What is my iniquity? And what is my sin before your father, that he is seeking my life?"
He said to him, "Far from it, you shall not die. Behold, my father does nothing either great or small without disclosing it to me. So why should my father hide this thing from me? It is not so!"

Yet David vowed again, saying, "Your father knows well that I have found favor in your sight, and he has said, 'Do not let Jonathan know this, or he will be grieved.' But truly as the Lord lives and as your soul lives, there is hardly a step between me and death."

*Then Jonathan said to David, "**Whatever you say, I will do for you.**"*

The emphasis on the last sentence is mine as I want to point out what an incredible statement this is from Jonathan to David. Jonathan is willing to do whatever it takes to help his friend. I can only imagine how David's heart must have been encouraged by these words from his friend.

But Jonathan is not done encouraging David yet. David comes up with a simple plan for Jonathan to let him know if King Saul is really intent on killing him and if he should flee.

Without getting into all the details, Jonathan follows the instructions given to him by David and is able to warn David that the King is indeed intent on killing him.

This is where Jonathan gives David some parting words of encouragement.

1 Samuel 20:42

Jonathan said to David, "Go in safety, inasmuch as we have sworn to each other in the name of the Lord, saying, 'The Lord will be between me and you, and between my descendants and your descendants forever.'" Then he rose and departed, while Jonathan went into the city.

Jonathan does not yet know at this time that David is going to be King one day. He only knows that David is his friend. He is basically telling David that he and his family will have nothing to fear in the future when he is King. What powerful and incredible words! What a great friendship.

King Saul is now hunting David and pursues him across the country side. He finally finds out that David appears to be in the Desert of Ziph and is closing in, ready to strike him down once and for all.

In this final act of friendship, Jonathan seeks out David to offer these words of encouragement.

1 Samuel 23:15-18

Now David became aware that Saul had come out to seek his life while David was in the wilderness of Ziph at Horesh. And Jonathan, Saul's son, arose and went to David at Horesh, and encouraged him in God. Thus he said to him, "Do not be afraid, because the hand of Saul my father will not find you, and you will be king over Israel and I will be next to you; and Saul my father knows that also." So the two of them made a covenant before the Lord; and David stayed at Horesh while Jonathan went to his house.

Jonathan now knows that he will not be King of Israel. That mantle has passed to David. When you think about it, all Jonathan has to do is kill David and he would be the next King. However, Jonathan chooses friendship, loyalty and love over his own personal desires for success. He also must know that God has anointed David and to harm the "anointed one" would be a very serious sin.

I hope that you have a Jonathan in your life; someone who can offer you love and encouragement, even when it might not be in their best interest. Someone who has "got your back" and will always be do things that are in your best interest.

Or perhaps, you can be the Jonathan in someone's' life.

Look for those opportunities to offer encouragement to others especially when they are in danger and facing great adversity. It is easy to be a friend in good times; it is much more difficult in times of trouble.

Barnabas & Saul

This is not King Saul of the Old Testament; this is Saul of the New Testament. This is Saul, who would one day become the Apostle Paul the prolific writer of the New Testament.

Saul was originally a bitter enemy of the early church and set out to destroy the church and anybody associated with it. He was there when Stephen became the first martyr and was stoned to death.

However, God had a plan to greatly use Saul to spread the good news of the Gospel of Jesus Christ.

On the road to Damascus (where Saul is headed to persecute Christians), he is blinded by the Lord and had to be led by hand into the city. For three days he was in this condition (I think it is very interesting that God choose three days for Saul to suffer - the same amount of time that Jesus spent from his death until his resurrection).

Can you image being blind for three days? Saul must have had plenty of time to pray, think, and contemplate his past life.

God is about to start encouraging Saul through two men who will come alongside him (even though many feared him because of his reputation).

Suddenly, God sends a disciple named Ananias to lay hands on Saul to heal him of his blindness. What joy and relief Saul must have felt. It was also a confirmation of the vision God had given him that a man named Ananias was going to help him.

Do you think Saul was encouraged? Do you think others around him were encouraged as well? Saul once was blind, but now he "sees" for the first time in his life.

Acts 9:26-28

So Ananias departed and entered the house, and after laying his hands on him said, "Brother Saul, the Lord Jesus, who appeared to you on the road by which you were coming, has sent me so that you may regain your sight and be filled with the Holy Spirit."

And immediately there fell from his eyes something like scales, and he regained his sight, and he got up and was baptized; and he took food and was strengthened.

Saul stays in Damascus for a short time, until his life is threatened and then he know he must flee.

Saul heads to Jerusalem and he tries to join the disciples and is hit with the reality of his past reputation.

They all feared him. Saul must have been crushed and very disappointed. He knew that he was a changed man, but he now had to deal with the consequences of his past deeds.

Lucky for Saul, there was a man there who was about to give him his greatest encouragement yet!

Acts 9:26-28

When he came to Jerusalem, he was trying to associate with the disciples; but they were all afraid of him, not believing that he was a disciple. But Barnabas took hold of him and brought him to the apostles and described to them how he had seen the Lord on the road, and that He had talked to him, and how at Damascus he had spoken out boldly in the name of Jesus. And he was with them, moving about freely in Jerusalem, speaking out boldly in the name of the Lord.

Notice how it says that Barnabas "took hold of him" and brought him to the apostles. Why did Barnabas have to take hold of him?

My guess is that Saul was dejected and did not want to go. He had tried it on his own and the people feared him. Why would anyone sign up for more rejection??

Barnabas went out a limb and spoke up for Saul. Not only did he "vouch" for him, but he praised him for his bold stance in Damascus for the cause of Christ.

Barnabas truly earned his nickname "son of encouragement" with these words to the apostles. Saul is sitting there in front of the apostle of Christ and here he is being spoken about positively.

Proverbs 27:2

Let another praise you, and not your own mouth; A stranger, and not your own lips

Saul's heart must have soared that day! God used Barnabas to speak encouragement into his life at a crucial time of his conversion.

Saul is sent home to Tarsus because of the threats to his life. Later Barnabas joins him for a year and they move to Antioch where the believers are first called Christians.

After that, Saul and Barnabas go on to make the first missionary journey together. What a great companion Barnabas must have been for Paul in those early years. God knew that Saul would need lots of encouragement as they faced many trials and obstacles as they preached and taught the Good News of Jesus Christ.

Saul eventually changes his name to Paul and takes a young disciple under his wing by the name of Timothy. Paul goes on to pen two letters of encouragement to Timothy (1st and 2nd Timothy in our bible). I would like to think that Paul's ability to encourage was a direct result of having been influenced by Barnabas. In other words he was "paying it forward".

Has someone encouraged you in your life? Have you thanked them lately? Is there someone you can encourage and "pay forward" the encouragement that was brought into your life?

Take the time now to thank God for those encouragers he has brought into your life.

Paul & Timothy

Have you ever had a mentor in your life?

Have you been a mentor to someone?

We all need positive mentors in our life to help guide and direct us on the right path.   A good mentor always has our best interest in mind and only wants to see us be successful and do well.   A good mentor is also not afraid to correct us and offer discipline when necessary.

Timothy was a young Christian who was positively influenced by both his mother and grandmother.   He also had a mentor in the apostle Paul.   Paul felt so close to Timothy that he referred to him as "son".

In the books of 1st and 2nd Timothy Paul offers much encouragement to Timothy.   As you read these words of encouragement, think of the many "Timothy's" in your life and how you can speak words of encouragement to them.

Paul tells Timothy to - Fight the good fight!

1 Timothy 1:18-19

This command I entrust to you, Timothy, my son, in accordance with the prophecies previously made concerning you, that by them you fight the good fight, keeping faith and a good conscience, which some have rejected and suffered shipwreck in regard to their faith.

Paul tells Timothy - Do not worry about what others think!

1 Timothy 4:12

Let no one look down on your youthfulness, but rather in speech, conduct, love, faith and purity, show yourself an example of those who believe.

Paul tells him again - Fight the good fight!

1 Timothy 6:12

Fight the good fight of faith; take hold of the eternal life to which you were called, and you made the good confession in the presence of many witnesses.

Paul encourages him - You have incredible faith!

2 Timothy 1:5

For I am mindful of the sincere faith within you, which first dwelt in your grandmother Lois and your mother Eunice, and I am sure that it is in you as well.

Paul tells Timothy - Be Strong!

2 Timothy 2:1-7

You therefore, my son, be strong in the grace that is in Christ Jesus. The things which you have heard from me in the presence of many witnesses, entrust these to faithful men who will be able to teach others also. Suffer hardship with me, as a good soldier of Christ Jesus. No soldier in active service entangles himself in the affairs of everyday life, so that he may please the one who enlisted him as a soldier. Also if anyone competes as an athlete, he does not win the prize unless he competes according to the rules. The hard-working farmer ought to be the first to receive his share of the crops. Consider what I say, for the Lord will give you understanding in everything.

Paul uses very powerful words to speak encouragement into Timothy's life. He does not pull any punches, but is loving and kind as he offers his advice and counsel.

The books for 1st and 2nd Timothy offer many more lesson and teaching beyond these few words for encouragement. Paul was very concerned with Timothy's spiritual growth and maturity and wants him to finish well.

I should note that all of these words are in the forms of letters that Paul had written to Timothy. He was not there in person, so he did the next best thing he could do at this time and that was to write a letter.

You should use every form of communication at your disposal when you are trying to encourage someone. Just because you are not with them in person, does not be you cannot encourage them.

My oldest daughter took the opportunity to write me a letter that she wanted me to open in the future. It was specifically labeled "Open when you really miss me". She is away at college, so I seldom see her these days. Then one day, I was very discouraged and was missing my daughter and I remembered her letter. I opened the letter and it was filled with love and encouragement. I wept tears of joy and happiness. My daughter was so thoughtful and of course the timing was perfect.

My hope and prayer is that you will fight the good fight and finish well. Look for the opportunity to be a mentor and pray that God would send a mentor into your life. We all need someone in our life to encourage, challenge and help us through this life.

Finally

It is impossible to encourage yourself. It takes someone coming along side you to bring you encouragement. Therefore, if you isolate yourself during times of crisis, you will miss the blessing of being encouraged.

One last thing.

It will be hard to imagine this as you are going through the trials and tribulations, but when you come out on the other side, you are the one who will be doing the encouraging. You will be able to reach out to someone else who is going through a similar circumstance and offer them words for advice and encouragement and tell them how God brought you through the situation.

I have found that many times in my life, God has used the circumstances of my life to speak into the life of someone else, IF I am willing and obedient to His call.

Encouraging Quotes

"If you want to lift yourself up, lift up someone else.
–Booker T. Washington

Believe you can and you're halfway there. –Theodore Roosevelt

"When you encourage others, you in the process are encouraged because you're making a commitment and difference in that person's life. Encouragement really does make a difference". Zig Ziglar

"Do what you can, where you are, with what you have."
Teddy Roosevelt

"A word of encouragement from a teacher to a child can change a life. A word of encouragement from a spouse can save a marriage. A word of encouragement from a leader can inspire a person to reach her potential."
John C. Maxwell

"Nothing is impossible, the word itself says, "I'm possible!" –Audrey Hepburn

"Nine tenths of education is encouragement."
Anatole France

"If you are a leader, you should never forget that everyone needs encouragement. And everyone who receives it - young or old, successful or less-than-successful, unknown or famous - is changed by it."
 John C. Maxwell

"Instruction does much, but encouragement everything."
— Johann Wolfgang von Goethe

Encouraging Quotes

"When you come to the end of your rope, tie a knot and hang on." - **Franklin D. Roosevelt**

"Don't be discouraged. It's often the last key in the bunch that opens the lock." - **Unknown**

"Whether you think you can or you think you can't, you're right." **Henry Ford**

"The difficulties of life are intended to make us better, not bitter." **Unknown**

"The pessimist sees difficulty in every opportunity. The optimist sees opportunity in every difficulty" - **Winston Churchill**

"Character cannot be developed in ease and quiet. Only through experience of trial and suffering can the soul be strengthened, ambition inspired, and success achieved." - **Helen Keller**

"If you're going through hell, keep going." -**Winston Churchill**

Praise & Worship

How do you praise and worship God in times of sorrow, agony, trial and tribulation? Is it even possible to do? What about a storm that literally sweeps your family away?

"Saved alone"

That is the cable that Horatio Spafford received from his wife in November of 1873.   The ship she was traveling on with their four daughters collided with another ship and sank. She alone survived the disaster.

The family had been mourning the loss of their son (and brother) and they we taking a trip to Europe to recover from that loss.   It was only a last minute business meeting that kept Horatio from joining his family on that fateful voyage.

As he hurried to England to console his grieving wife, he penned the words to an incredible hymn.   You can only imagine what was going through his mind as he traveled the same waters that swept away his precious children.   He was a man of deep faith and conviction and the words are as fresh today as they were almost 150 years ago.

Take the time to slowly read the words, remember the context and consider the faith of the man who wrote this beautiful and powerful hymn.   Let it touch your mind, body and soul.

It Is Well With My Soul

When peace, like a river, attendeth my way,
When sorrows like sea billows roll;
Whatever my lot, Thou hast taught me to say,
It is well, it is well with my soul.

Refrain:

It is well (it is well),
With my soul (with my soul),
It is well, it is well with my soul.

Though Satan should buffet, though trials should come,
Let this blest assurance control,
That Christ hath regarded my helpless estate,
And hath shed His own blood for my soul.

Refrain

My sin, oh the bliss of this glorious thought!
My sin, not in part but the whole,
Is nailed to His cross, and I bear it no more,
Praise the Lord, praise the Lord, O my soul!

Refrain

For me, be it Christ, be it Christ hence to live:
If Jordan above me shall roll,
No pang shall be mine, for in death as in life
Thou wilt whisper Thy peace to my soul.

Refrain

And Lord haste the day, when my faith shall be sight,
The clouds be rolled back as a scroll;
The trump shall resound, and the Lord shall descend,
Even so, it is well with my soul.

Refrain

The loss of a loved one is perhaps the hardest thing to overcome and deal with in our life. To lose all of your children could be devastating and debilitating, but Horatio chose to rise above the grief and sorrow and worship God.

Most of us will never have to deal with something this terrible, but we will all have to deal with trials, troubles and tribulations in our life. We will all come face to face with that time when we have to make a choice as to whether or not our faith will rocked to its foundation, or if we will CHOOSE to praise and worship God.

The only way to prepare is to seek God's face daily in your own time of study, prayer, praise and worship. Just as an athlete must exercise every day to prepare his mind and body for the competition to come, we must exercise our heart and mind and fill them with God's words and promises. There is no shortcut to preparation.

Choose today to be student of the Bible.

As you continue through this chapter, it is my hope and prayer that you will get a keen sense of the power of praise and worship and realize that God is worthy of our praise – all the time.

Finally – every time I proof read this section of the book, I would pull up this song on the internet and listen to it. It speaks so clearly to my soul as I listen to it. I cannot help raising my hands, singing along and praising God!

Choosing to Worship God by his Attributes

I read an excellent article by Bob Hostetler that was entitled: *31 Ways to Praise: Creating A Vocabulary of Praise.* He was kind enough to allow me to include it in this book.

In the article, Bob talks about how he is influenced by a book written by Cecil ("Cec") Murphey - <u>*Invading the Privacy of God,*</u> and how he developed a list of 31 ways to praise God. It was a systematic way to praise and pray. I thought this was a brilliant idea and wanted to share his idea on how you can praise God based on his attributes. This would prove most helpful even when you do not "feel "like praising God.

What follows is the article Bob published:

31 Ways to Praise:
Creating A Vocabulary of Praise
by Bob Hostetler

I'm not often at a loss for words. My wife says that, when we first began dating, my use of words to describe her considerable charms was one of the things that most encouraged her budding love for me. Later, as a pastor and preacher, I seldom struggled for something to say, either in or out of the pulpit. And, of course, as a writer, my long-time friendship with words has stood me in good stead (after all, writers are often paid by the word!).

But it's always been different, it seems, in prayer. Though I don't exchange small talk very well, I can usually hold up my end of the conversation without difficulty. . . except when it comes to prayer, and particularly when I undertake to express my praise to God.

I ordinarily try to begin and end my prayer times with praise and adoration. But most of the time, I'm flat out speechless. I want to praise God with all that is within me, but my tongue seems to halt in my mouth, and I can't think of a sensible thing to say.

That was the case, at least, until recently, when I read a book by a friend of mine, Cecil ("Cec") Murphey. Cec's excellent book, invading the Privacy of God, described his habit of praying according to a list of God's attributes. He described how his prayer life was revolutionized when he settled on the practice of concentrating on God as the Wonderful Counselor one day, the Mighty God the second day, the Everlasting Father the next day, and the Prince of Peace the following day (Isaiah 9:6). Some days, he revealed, he would praise God for being a refuge in times of trouble (Psalm 46:1); other days he would focus on God's faithfulness (Lamentations 3:23).

Cec's concept opened a door to new power in praise for me. I began imitating his practice, applying it specifically to the moments in my prayer life when I want to focus on praising God for who he is. Over the course of a few months, I developed a "program of praise" that has proven wonderfully helpful to me in expressing my praise to my praiseworthy God.

Since I've been using the following list, praise for God has begun to flow freely from my heart and from my lips during my prayer times, as I focus on one attribute of my awesome God and Father each day, and use the Scripture-based sentences as "praise-starters." At the end of each month, I begin praying through the list all over again, sometimes combining traits when the month is shorter than thirty-one days.

Whether you adopt or adapt the following, or compose a praise program of your own, I pray that this suggested "praise program" may help your praise ascend plentifully and purposefully to God in ways that will make the angels blush with envy!

1. **God the Creator** "Creator God, I praise you because you made the heavens, even the highest heavens, and all their starry host, the earth and all that is on it, the seas and all that is in them. You give life to everything, and the multitudes of heaven worship you'. . . " (Neh. 9:6).

2. **The Only God** "God, I praise you because you are the LORD, and there is no other; apart from you there is no God. . . " (Isaiah 45:5).

3. **The Almighty God** "O LORD God Almighty, who is like you? You are mighty, O LORD," and I praise you . . ." (Psalm 89:8).

4. **The Everlasting Father**, the Ancient of Days "I praise you, Lord, as the Ancient of Days (Daniel 7:9), the Everlasting Father (Isaiah 9:6), who lives forever and ever. . . ."

5. **A Loving God** "I praise you because you are a loving God, whose very nature is love. . . ." (1 John 4:16).

6. **A God of Justice** "Lord, I praise and magnify you, who is just and the one who justifies those who have faith in Jesus. . . ." (Romans 3:26).

7. **The Trustworthy God** "Heavenly Father, I give you my praise and adoration, because you are a "faithful God, keeping [your] covenant of love to a thousand generations of those who love [you] and keep [your] commands. . . ." (Deuteronomy 7:9).

8. **A Merciful God** "You, O Lord, are a gracious and merciful God," (Nehemiah 9:31), and I praise you for your great mercy. . . ."

9. **God my Refuge, my Fortress** "I praise you, Lord, for you are my mighty rock, my refuge. . . .'" (Psalm 62:7).

10. **A Longsuffering, Persevering God** "Father, I praise you because you are patient with [all your children], not wanting anyone to perish, but everyone to come to repentance' (2 Pet. 3:9).Thank you for your patience with me. . . ."

11. **The Only Wise God** "I give praise to you, my Father, the only wise God [my] Saviour' (Jude 1:25). May all glory and majesty, dominion and power, be yours both now and ever. . . ."

12. **The Holy One** "Holy, holy, holy are you, Lord God Almighty, who was, and is, and is to come. . .." (Revelation 4:8).

13. **A Personal God** "I praise you, God, because you are a personal God, who gives me the honor of knowing you personally, just like you did to Abraham, Isaac, and Jacob. . . ." (Matthew 8:11).

14. **A Giving God** "Praise and honor be yours, O God, because you are a generous God, who did not even stop short of giving your own Son (John 3:16). . . ."

15. **The Provider God** "I praise you today, Lord, as my Jehovah-jireh, who will generously provide all [I] need'. . . " (2 Corinthians 9:7).

16. **The Shepherd God** "I bless your name and praise you as my Jehovah-rohi, who will shepherd me and guide me in the paths of righteousness for your name's sake" (Psalm 23:1-3).

17. **God my Victory** "Praise to you, my God, because you are my Jehovah-nissi, God my victory, who always leads [me] in triumphal procession in Christ'. . . ." (2 Corinthians 2:14)

18. **God my Peace** "I praise you with all my heart, Lord, because you are my Jehovah-shalom, the God of peace [who] will soon crush Satan under [my] feet. . . ." (Romans 16:20).

19. **The God Who Heals** "Father, I praise you because you are the Lord who heals me. . . ." (Exodus 15:26).

20. **The God of All Comfort** "Praise be to the God and Father of our Lord Jesus Christ, the Father of compassion and the God of all comfort. . . ." (2 Corinthians 1:3).

21. **The God of Miracles** "Lord, I praise you because You are the God who performs miracles; you display your power among the people'. . . ." (Psalm 77:14).

22. **A Forgiving God** "I want to bless you with my praise, Father, because you are a forgiving God, gracious and compassionate, slow to anger and abounding in love'. . . ." (Nehemiah 9:17)

23. **The Burden-Bearer** "Praise be to the LORD, to God [my] Savior, who daily bears [my] burdens'. . . ." (Psalm 68:19).

24. **A Faithful God** "I praise you because your love, O LORD, reaches to the heavens, your faithfulness to the skies'. . . Great is your faithfulness'. . . ." (Psalm 36:5; Lamentations 3:23).

25. **God the Blessed and Only Ruler**, King of kings and Lord of lords "All honor and praise be to you, my God, the blessed and only Ruler, the King of kings and Lord of lords'. . . ." (1 Timothy 6:15).

26. **God the Liberator** "I praise you because You are my help and my deliverer; O LORD'. . . ." (Psalm 70:5).

27. **The Lifter of My Head** "Father God, I praise you because you are a shield around me, O LORD; you bestow glory on me and lift up my head' when I am weary or depressed. . . ." (Psalm 3:3).

28. **A God of Light** "I praise you, Lord, because you are my light and my salvation,' and because you know what lies in darkness, and light dwells with you'. . . ." (Psalm 27:1, Daniel 2:22).

29. **A God of Joy** "I give you my praise, O Lord, because you have granted [me] eternal blessings and made me glad with the joy of your presence'. . . ." (Psalm 21:6).

30. **The God Who Answers Prayer** "I praise and honor you, Father, because you are a God who loves to answer prayer, and who begins to answer even before I begin to pray" (Isaiah 65:24).

31. **The God of All the Earth** "I praise and adore you, Lord, as the Holy One of Israel. . . [my] Redeemer. . . the God of all the earth'. . . ." (Isaiah 54:5).

It may seem simple, but this "praise program" has energized my "praise life," helping me to praise God more knowledgeably and purposefully in prayer. It has also enlarged my vision and awareness of the praiseworthy God I love and serve and, I believe, increased the evidence of his godly character in my life. My prayer is that it may begin to do the same for you as well.

Copyright Bob Hostetler (www.bobhostetler.com). Used with the permission of the author. A related prayer plan ("31 Ways to Pray for Your Kids") is available as an iPhone/iPad app in the iTunes app store.

This has really helped me as well in those time of stress and trouble to be able to take the focus off of me and put the focus on God and praising Him.   He is worthy of our praise all the time.

When you are in the valley, in the depths of despair, lean into God and his goodness and mediate on those attributes that make him our Lord and Creator.

You can take one of these characteristics for each day of the week and pray over, praise and meditate upon the attributes of God.

Paul and Silas Imprisoned

What if you were wrongly accused, beaten and imprisoned? I don't know about you, but I think I would be pretty discouraged and not in much of a mood to praise or worship.   I would most likely be wallowing in self-pity and wondering "why me O' Lord?"

However, this is exactly what happens to Paul and Silas as they were traveling through Macedonia.   Paul had been called to European continent to bring the Good news of the Gospel of Jesus Christ to the people there.

Paul was annoyed because a slave girl with an evil spirit of divination had been following then around and proclaiming the work they were doing.   Paul commanded the spirt to come out of the girl and her master as upset because he knew that he could no longer use her to make money (it's always about the money – never mind that this poor girl was healed).

They were arrested, beaten and thrown in jail. Not only that, they were put in stocks (very uncomfortable and completely confining). This all happened without the benefit of a trial – which they were afforded since they were Roman citizens.

Read the account below as we pick up the story from Acts 16:22-30

The crowd rose up together against them, and the chief magistrates tore their robes off them and proceeded to order them to be beaten with rods. When they had struck them with many blows, they threw them into prison, commanding the jailer to guard them securely; and he, having received such a command, threw them into the inner prison and fastened their feet in the stocks.

But about midnight Paul and Silas were praying and singing hymns of praise to God, and the prisoners were listening to them; and suddenly there came a great earthquake, so that the foundations of the prison house were shaken; and immediately all the doors were opened and everyone's chains were unfastened. When the jailer awoke and saw the prison doors opened, he drew his sword and was about to kill himself, supposing that the prisoners had escaped. But Paul cried out with a loud voice, saying, "Do not harm yourself, for we are all here!" And he called for lights and rushed in, and trembling with fear he fell down before Paul and Silas, and after he brought them out, he said, "Sirs, what must I do to be saved?"

You see, God has a deeper purpose for the path we must sometimes follow. In this case, the path through prison for Paul and Silas, lead to the path of salvation for the Jailer and his family. Many have speculated that Paul and Silas were not only praising and worshiping God, but were most likely actively sharing the Gospel with all who could hear them. After all, they had a captive audience! Including the jailer.

The jailer was ready to end his life because in those times, if a prisoner escaped, then the jailer would be executed! The jailer was sure that his life was over. But praise God, his life was just about to begin as he is saved, baptized and born again. In verses 31 and following you can read the account of how the jailer and his entire household accept Jesus as their Lord and Savior.

Acts 16:31-34

They said, "Believe in the Lord Jesus, and you will be saved, you and your household." And they spoke the word of the Lord to him together with all who were in his house. And he took them that very hour of the night and washed their wounds, and immediately he was baptized, he and all his household. And he brought them into his house and set food before them, and rejoiced greatly, having believed in God with his whole household.

So here is the essential question - Would Paul and Silas have chosen this path? Probably not! Who would willingly sign up to be beaten and imprisoned? While they probably would not have chosen those circumstances, they certainly could choose their attitudes and actions that followed. This is the state of Christian maturity that we all need to strive for in our lives. To view our circumstances through the same prism that God views them. To not ask "why me", or "how come, but to ask "how will you use this in my life or the life of others to bring honor and glory Your name"?

Is this easy to do?

No, but now let us consider a man who lost almost everything and see how he chooses to react

What did JOB do in the midst of the storm?

I had introduced Job earlier in this book, but want to bring his story back again, because it is so powerful and his attitude and actions are so incredible.

Life is just wonderful!. You have a bunch of stuff you can check off your list:

- ✓ You have an incredible wife
- ✓ Wonderful children
- ✓ Business is doing very well
- ✓ You have good health
- ✓ Your relationship with God is really good.

What could possibly go wrong?

Most people would say you "had it made"!

Then your world gets turned upside down.

- You lose your business and your employees are slaughtered
- All of your children are killed
- Your health declines rapidly
- Your relationship with your wife is fragile.

What would be your frame of mind at this time? I have to believe that I would be a mess. I would probably be angry, sad, depressed and hurt.

This is where Job has found himself. His story is one that few of us could endure.

We pick up the story in the book of Job where he is described as blameless and upright. He has 10 children, 10,000 + animals and a multitude of servants. In other words, he is rich and blessed.

Then in a series of tests, he loses everything.

First raiders come and steal all of his animals, and then all of his children are killed by a powerful storm. Yet he does not sin or blame God.

In fact, see how he reacts to the disaster, it is really quite incredible!

Job 1:20-22

Then Job arose and tore his robe and shaved his head, and he fell to the ground and worshiped. He said,

"Naked I came from my mother's womb,
And naked I shall return there.
The Lord gave and the Lord has taken away.
Blessed be the name of the Lord."

Through all this Job did not sin nor did he blame God.

The bible says that he worshiped God! What a powerful testimony to his life and relationship with God. He lost it all, and yet he knew that all he needed was God. He knew that God was there with him in the beginning, he knew God was with him then and he knew God would be with him at the end of his days. It is a great reminder to us that God is enough!

God gave us this great story to not help us understand the HE is God and we are not. He did not explain himself to Job! He is the master and creator of the universe. He can see end to end and from horizon to horizon. Only He knows His reasons and why He is allowing circumstances to come into our life. It is our role to submit to His perfect will and way for our life and praise and worship Him no matter what.

James 5:11

We count those blessed who endured. You have heard of the endurance of Job and have seen the outcome of the Lord's dealings that the Lord is full of compassion and is merciful.

Who, What, When, Where, Why, & How of Praise

Now I would like us to exam the different aspects of praise. The answers really should not surprise you at all. If anything, it is a gentle reminder to all of us in regards to praise.

I want to dive in the following questions:

Q. Who Should Praise God?
A. Everybody & Everything

Q. What is Praise?
A. Praise is an outward expression of the inner faith we have in God.

Q. When should we Praise God?
A. All the time!

Q. Where should we praise God?
A. Everywhere!

Q. Why should we praise God?
A. He is worthy!

Q. How should we praise God?
A. It is a full body experience!

———

Who should praise God?

The answer is quite simple really:

- Everybody (including angels and heavenly hosts)
- Everything

Psalm 150:6

Let everything that has breath praise the Lord. Praise the Lord!

This should not come as a shock to you, but we are all called to Praise God. We are meant to praise God and his is worthy of our praise.

As Jesus was entering Jerusalem on the young donkey and all of the people were praising him and praising God, the Pharisees, admonished him and asked him to make the people stop their praise. This is what Jesus had to say to them:

Luke 19:40

But Jesus answered, "I tell you, if these become silent, the stones will cry out!"

Wouldn't that be incredible if the rocks and hills were to cry out praises to God almighty! Let's hope the day never comes when we stop praising God and the stones have to call out.

Psalm 66:4

"All the earth will worship You,
And will sing praises to You;
They will sing praises to Your name."   *Selah.*

All of creation is commanded to praise and worship God. Who are we to deny God the praise and worship He so richly deserves.

What is Praise?

In its simplest form, Praise is an outward expression of the inner faith we have in God.   Praise is also a sacrifice we make to God (Heb 13:15).

There are a number of words in the bible that are used to express praise to God

Halal is a primary Hebrew root word for praise. Our word "hallelujah" comes from this base word. It means "to be clear, to shine, to boast, show, to rave, celebrate, to be clamorously foolish."

Yadah is a verb with a root meaning, "the extended hand, to throw out the hand, therefore to worship with extended hand." According to the Lexicon, the opposite meaning is "to bemoan, the wringing of the hands."

Towdah comes from the same principle root word as yadah, but is used more specifically. Towdah literally means, "an extension of the hand in adoration, avowal, or acceptance." By way of application, it is apparent in the Psalms and elsewhere that it is used for thanking God for "things not yet received" as well as things already at hand.

Shabach means, "to shout, to address in a loud tone, to command, to triumph."

Barak means "to kneel down, to bless God as an act of adoration."

Zamar means "to pluck the strings of an instrument, to sing, to praise; a musical word which is largely involved with joyful expressions of music with musical instruments.

Tehillah is derived from the word halal and means "the singing of halals, to sing or to laud; perceived to involve music, especially singing; hymns of the Spirit.

https://buddysheets.tripod.com/hebrewwordsforpraise.htm

When Should We Praise God?

When should we praise God? This is more about the timing of our praise .vs the circumstances (which we discussed earlier in the book). Here is what I found:

- **Morning** - Psalm 92:1-2, 1 Chronicles 23:30
- **Night** - Acts 16:25
- **Praise should be continuous** - Psalm 34:1, Heb. 13:15
- **Every day we should praise** God - Psalm 61:8
- **Three times a day!** - Daniel 6:10
- **Seven times per day**! - Psalm 119:164
- **Forever** - Psalm 145: 1-2
- **All day long** - Psalm 71:8

Is there a bad time to praise God? NO!   Paul and Silas praised God at Midnight in jail.

Is there a good time to praise God? YES! All the time

I know it is very obvious, but it really does not matter what time of day it is.   We can praise God 24 hours per day.   He is always there and ready to receive our praise and worship. Don't wait until Sunday when you are in Church to praise God. Look for opportunities all the day long to praise Him. Most importantly, prepare your heart, mind, body and soul to praise him in those times of Trial, Troubles and Tribulations, because we never know when those will come.

Where Should We Praise God?

I think David gives us some good insight from Psalm 139 as to where we should praise God. Then answer as you have probably guessed is EVERYWHERE! There is no place we can go and God will not be there with us. Therefore, no matter where we are, we can praise and worship God there.

Read Psalm 139 to better understand that there is no place we can go that God won't be with us and that we can offer praise everywhere

Psalm 139: 7-14

Where can I go from Your Spirit?
Or where can I flee from Your presence?
If I ascend to heaven, You are there;
If I make my bed in Sheol, behold, You are there.
If I take the wings of the dawn,
If I dwell in the remotest part of the sea,
Even there Your hand will lead me,
And Your right hand will lay hold of me.
If I say, "Surely the darkness will overwhelm me,
And the light around me will be night,"
Even the darkness is not dark to You,
And the night is as bright as the day.
Darkness and light are alike to You.
For You formed my inward parts;
You wove me in my mother's womb.
I will give thanks to You, for I am fearfully and wonderfully made;
Wonderful are Your works,
And my soul knows it very well.

Why Should We Praise God?

As I was thinking about why we should praise God, I was constantly driven to the Psalms and the incredible insight and praise that is offered there.   As I considered which Psalms to include in the chapter, I came across the following work from Melissa Deming.   She has been writing and blogging for a number of years and you can find her work at hiveresources.com.   She was kind enough to allow me to include the work as part of this chapter. Below is her insight into Psalm 145:

Psalm 145 gives us 22 reasons to praise God – all based on who God is and what he does for us. That's almost as many reasons as verses in the chapter!

Listen to why the Psalmist says we should praise God even when we don't feel like it:

> *God is a personal God (vs. 1)*
> *God is the sovereign King (vs. 2)*
> *God is great (vs. 3)*
> *God is unsearchable (vs. 3)*
> *God acts on my behalf (vs. 4)*
> *God is majestic (vs. 5)*
> *God is good (vs. 6)*
> *God is righteous (vs. 7)*
> *God is gracious (vs. 8)*
> *God is full of compassion (vs. 8)*
> *God is slow to anger (vs. 8)*
> *God is merciful (vs. 8)*
> *God is powerful (vs. 10)*
> *God makes himself known to me (vs. 11)*
> *God helps me (vs. 14)*
> *God provides for me (vs. 15)*
> *God is generous (vs. 16)*
> *God is near to me (vs. 18)*
> *God listens to me (vs. 19)*
> *God saves me (vs. 19)*
> *God preserves me (vs. 20)*
> *God brings justice (vs. 21)*

Maybe Ps. 145 should be subtitled – "Praises for the Tongue-Tied Worshipper."

Especially considering that it was Jewish practice to recite this very psalm three times a day – twice in the morning and once in the evening![1]

Does life have you tongue-tied? Pick up David's song of praise in Ps. 145 and make it your own. We have much to praise Him for! 22 reasons to be exact!

Imagine the impact on your heart if you recited this passage three times a day!

[1] VanGemeren, Willem A. "Psalm 145: Great Is Yahweh's Universal Kingdom!" In The Expositor's Bible Commentary: Volume 5. 860. Grand Rapids: Zondervan Publishing House, © 1991.

What great insight into God's word! Melissa found the keen insight that Jewish practice was to recite this Psalm 3 times per day. I would be a good idea for you to bookmark this Psalm in you bible, on your phone if you have a bible app or to print out the Psalm and keep it handy. If you have children, this might be a good Psalm to read each evening before you go to sleep. What a great way to teach our children about why we should praise and honor God.

Take time to stop right now and read this psalm and mediate on the words and then offer a prayer of praise and worship to our great and wonderful God.

Beyond Psalm 145, there are plenty of other verses in the bible that give us reasons as to why we should praise God because:

- He is Great
- He is Worthy of praise

Psalm 96:4

For great is the Lord and greatly to be praised;
He is to be feared above all gods.

2 Samuel 22:4

"I call upon the Lord, who is worthy to be praised,
And I am saved from my enemies.

Psalm 18:3

I call upon the Lord, who is worthy to be praised,
And I am saved from my enemies.

Psalm 100:3-4

Know that the Lord Himself is God;
It is He who has made us, and not we ourselves;
We are His people and the sheep of His pasture.
Enter His gates with thanksgiving
And His courts with praise.
Give thanks to Him, bless His name.

Revelation 4:11

"Worthy are You, our Lord and our God, to receive glory and honor and
power; for You created all things, and because of Your will they existed, and
were created."

How are we to praise God?

Praising God is a full body experience! We are called to praise God with our voice – singing and shouting praise. With our arms and hands –clapping and hands held high. With our feet and legs dancing, twirling and leaping and praising Him. We can also play musical instruments such as the trumpet, harp, lyre, timbrel, stringed instruments, pipe and loud cymbals.   Read Psalm 150 and you will get real sense of how to Praise God.

You get the sense the God does not care so much "how" we praise him, but "that" we praise him!

We see in the Lord's Prayer he was teaching his disciples that you should begin and end with praise to God. This is true not only for prayer but for every aspect of our lives.

Matthew 6:9-13

"Pray, then, in this way:
'Our Father who is in heaven,
Hallowed be Your name.
'Your kingdom come.
Your will be done,
On earth as it is in heaven.
'Give us this day our daily bread.
'And forgive us our debts, as we also have forgiven our debtors.
'And do not lead us into temptation, but deliver us from evil. For Yours is
the kingdom and the power and the glory forever. Amen.'

There are many different ways for us to offer Biblical expressions of Praise to God:

Praising God in Psalms

The Psalmist knew how to Praise God!   A number of the Psalms start with words of praise to God.   This is not an accident,

Each of the following verses start a particular Psalm.

Many of these Psalms were written by David.   A man who knew much tragedy and sorrow in his life.   He was tried and tested in many areas of his life and yet he was able to praise and worship God in spite of his circumstances.

Let these verses wash over you and see how often they start by praising God.   This is a good lesson for us to start our conversations to God with praise.

O Lord, our Lord, how majestic is your name in all the earth! 8:1

I will praise you, O Lord with all my heart; 9:1

I will exalt you, O Lord, for you lifted me out of the depths: 30:1

I will extol the Lord at all times; his praise will always be on my lips. 34:1

Great is the Lord, and most worthy of Praise, 48:1

It is good to praise the Lord and make music to you name, O Most High. 92:1

I will sing of you love and justice; to you O Lord, I will sing praise, 101:1

Praise the Lord, O my soul; all my inmost being, praise his holy name. 103:1

Praise the Lord, O my soul. O Lord my God, you are very great; you are clothed with splendor and majesty. 104:1

Praise the Lord. I will extol the Lord with all my heart in the council of the upright and in the assembly.   111:1

Praise the Lord. Blessed is the man who fears the Lord, who finds great delight in his commands. 112:1

Praise the Lord. Praise, O servants of the Lord, praise the name of the Lord. 113:1

Praise the Lord, all you nation; extol him all you peoples. 117:1

Praise the Lord, all you servants of the Lord, who minister by night in the house of the Lord. 134:1

Praise the Lord. Praise the name of the Lord; praise him, you servants of the Lord. 135:1

I will praise you, O Lord, with all my heart; before the "gods" I will sing your praise. 138:1

Praise be to the Lord my Rock, who trains my hand for ware, my fingers for battle. 144:1

I will exalt you, by God the King; I will praise you name for ever and ever, 145:1

Praise the Lord. Praise the Lord, O my soul. 146:1

Praise the Lord. How good is it to sing praise to our God, how pleasant and fitting to praise him! 147:1

Praise the Lord. Praise the Lord form the heavens, praise him in the heights above. 148:1

Praise the Lord. Sing to the Lord a new song, his praise in the assembly of the saints. 149:1

Praise the Lord. Praise God in his sanctuary; praise him in his mighty heavens. 150:1

Note how they are praising God:

They Praise Him with their lips,
They Praise Him with their hearts,
They Praise Him with music,
They Praise Him with song,
They Praise him from the heights,
They Praise Him from the depths,
They Praise Him because He is worthy!

What we have seen from these examples is that we can and should continue to praise and worship God no matter what the circumstances are in our life. It will probably not be easy, and there will be friends and family who may call you crazy, but our God is great and greatly to be praised.

Finally, as I had stated in the very beginning of this book, it is not a question of "if" you will have trials, tribulations and tragedy in your life. It only a question of when and how often.

To that end you can prepare your attitude and actions by memorizing scripture that will help you in those desperate times. It is God's very word that will help to comfort and console you and bring the peace that passes all understanding.

Quotes on Praise and Worship

"Worship is the submission of all our nature to God. It is the quickening of conscience by His holiness, the nourishment of the mind with His truth, the purifying of the imagination of His beauty, the opening of the heart to His love, the surrender of the will to His purpose." William Temple

"The most valuable thing the Psalms do for me is to express the same delight in God which made David dance." C.S. Lewis

"Worship is the believer's response of all that they are – mind, emotions, will, body – to what God is and says and does." Warren Wiersbe

"The climax of God's happiness is the delight He takes in the echoes of His excellence in the praises of His people." John Piper

"Without worship, we go about miserable." A. W. Tozer

"It is in the process of being worshipped that God communicates His presence to men." C.S. Lewis

"No chorus is too loud, no orchestra too large, no Psalm too lofty for the lauding of the Lord of Hosts." Charles Spurgeon

"We would worry less if we praised more. Thanksgiving is the enemy of discontent and dissatisfaction." Harry Ironside

"Prayer and praise are the oars by which a man may row his boat into the deep waters of the knowledge of Christ." Charles Spurgeon

"Every good gift that we have had from the cradle up has come from God. If a man just stops to think what he has to praise God for, he will find there is enough to keep him singing praises for a week." D.L. Moody

---

Chapter Recap

So what have we learned about praise and worship in times of trials, troubles and tribulation?

✓ **Praise and Worship is a choice we make**

✓ **We can choose to praise God based on His character even when we do not feel like praising Him.**

✓ **<u>Who</u> should praise God?** Everyone and Everything

✓ **<u>What</u> is praise?** Praise is an outward expression of the inner faith we have in God.

✓ **<u>Where</u> should we praise God?** Everywhere

✓ **<u>When</u> should we praise God?** All the time

✓ **<u>Why</u> should we praise God?** Because He is worthy of praise

✓ **<u>How</u> should we praise God?** With our heart, mind, body and soul

Scripture to Memorize

1 Thessalonians 5:16-18

Rejoice always; pray without ceasing; in everything give thanks; for this is God's will for you in Christ Jesus.

Ephesians 5:20

Always giving thanks for all things in the name of our Lord Jesus Christ to God, even the Father;

Psalm 34:1

I will bless the Lord at all times;
His praise shall continually be in my mouth.

Philippians 4:7

And the peace of God, which surpasses all comprehension, will guard your hearts and your minds in Christ Jesus.

Joshua 1:9

Have I not commanded you? Be strong and courageous! Do not tremble or be dismayed, for the Lord your God is with you wherever you go."

James 1:2-4

Consider it all joy, my brethren, when you encounter various trials, knowing that the testing of your faith produces endurance. And let endurance have its perfect result, so that you may be perfect and complete, lacking in nothing.

Philippians 4:4

Rejoice in the Lord always; again I will say, rejoice!

Two Things You Control

When you are in that situation and you don't know what to do, know that there are two key areas of your life that you absolutely have control over:

- **Your Attitude**
- **Your Actions**

In my own life I am learning to praise God no matter what!   As I have been writing this book I was able to experience a personal example of God working through my life in a very simple way to help me control my attitude and actions.

I love to run.   I have been running for over 40 years and I cannot remember a time in my life when I could not run or did not want to run.   However, I cannot run right now.

I have spent the last two months (July and August in the Georgia), preparing myself for racing in the fall.   I have been dragging myself out of bed before the sun comes up to beat the heat and humidity. I was putting in 45-50 miles per week and preparing my mind and body to do speed training in the fall and then racing.

I was in the best shape I have been in a long time and was quite proud of my progress.

Then I injured my leg.

It was just a tweak at first but it lingered and lingered. Finally, it got to the point that I could not run at all.

It was on an early Monday morning when I injured my hamstring on my left leg. I was doing ¼ mile repeats at a very fast pace and it was on the eighth one that my leg was injured.

I followed the prescribed method of injury recovery.

RICE – Rest, Ice, Compression and Elevation.

If you know me, I hate to rest!!! I am constantly in motion. Having to lie still is incredibly difficult for me, but I knew this was the right thing to do.

I rested for 4 days and them went for a short run and felt ok. It was the next day that I tried to run and my leg just shut down after 10 minutes!

I wish I could say that I had the right attitude and actions for that first ½ hour, but I did not. I was frustrated and aggravated. I was angry and sad. I knew that my running was done for a long while and all the work and effort of the previous months was down the drain.

However, after that initial ½ hour of my pity party, I chose to praise God! I chose to worship God! I chose to thank God! It was an act of the will and it was all about changing my attitude.

I thanked God for:

1. The ability to walk
2. The ability to enjoy a beautiful day
3. The ability to fellowship with my bride and children
4. I thanked God for slowing me down and allowing my body to rest

My actions were reflected in how I shared the story with family and friend. I did not reflect on what had happened but look towards the future and what God will be bringing into my life.

Writing this book and doing the research helped me immensely in choosing to have a gratitude attitude and not wallowing for days in self-pity and frustration.   My only regret is that I had any doubts and frustration at all.   I wish that from the moment of the injury I had called out to God in praise and worship.   If nothing else, this injury has helped me to mature myself and make me a better man.

I know this is a very simplistic example and not very traumatic, but for me it was a great lesson and hopefully a turning point in my maturity and walk with the Lord.

Take a minute to consider your own circumstances right now and ask yourself about your own attitude and actions you have taken.

Here is the story of three guys who had both the right attitude and actions, in spite of their dire circumstances.

Shadrach, Meshach, and Abednego

Talk about trouble! Your country is invaded (most likely you have had friends and relatives killed in the battles) and you get carted off to a foreign land as bounty to the king.

Not only are you stripped of you nationality, you are even given a new name and forced to learn the language and customs of your captors.

This is the situation we find Hananiah, Mishael and Azariah – now these names are not nearly as familiar as the names there were given by their captors - Shadrach, Meshach, and Abednego (or if you are a fan of Veggie Tales – Rack, Shack and Benny).

These three young men find themselves in a foreign land and yet they choose to continue to worship their God and retain their Jewish heritage. They are captives of the Babylonians and it is King Nebuchadnezzar who had ordered them brought out of their land into Babylon.

The good news is that the king was really impressed with these guys and wants them to come work directly for him in his personal service, the bad news is that they are captives in a foreign land, so it's not like they had a lot of choice in the matter.

The king decides to make a golden statue and commands all of the people to fall down and worship this golden idol. Oh, and by the way there is one small consideration if you don't bow down and worship – you immediately get thrown in a huge oven and get burned to death.

Let's pick up the story from there in Daniel Chapter 3

Daniel 3:6

But whoever does not fall down and worship shall immediately be cast into the midst of a furnace of blazing fire."

So it is pretty unequivocal what the king wants. He wants everybody to worship this idol. It will also be pretty easy to see who is not worshiping the idol, because they will be the ones standing while everybody else is falling to their faces (in fear of death instead of worship to this idol).

Shadrach, Meshach, and Abednego refuse to worship this idol and are called out by others in the king's court. The kings is considerably angry and brings them in for questioning. He is going to give them one last chance before he lowers the "boom".

Daniel 3:15

"Now if you are ready, at the moment you hear the sound of the horn, flute, lyre, trigon, psaltery and bagpipe and all kinds of music, to fall down and worship the image that I have made, very well. But if you do not worship, you will immediately be cast into the midst of a furnace of blazing fire; and what god is there who can deliver you out of my hands?"

I love their reply to the king. It brings with it - confidence, hope, adoration and worship all wrapped together

Daniel 3:16-18

Shadrach, Meshach and Abednego replied to the king, "O Nebuchadnezzar, we do not need to give you an answer concerning this matter. If it be so, our God whom we serve is able to deliver us from the furnace of blazing fire; and He will deliver us out of your hand, O king. But even if He does not, let it be known to you, O king, that we are not going to serve your gods or worship the golden image that you have set up."

What happens to them? They are thrown in the fiery furnace! It heated to a temperature that was so hot and they king was so mad that the soldiers who cast them into the furnace perished because they acted so quickly.

In the end God, did deliver them from the fiery furnace and the King declared that nobody would say anything offensive about the God of Shadrach, Meshach, and Abednego.

Their attitude and actions in this situation are cause for celebration! They have a clear choice set before them and they choose to do the right thing, in spite of the consequences.

<u>Action</u> – speak up and stand up against evil

<u>Attitude</u> – we do not care what happens to us because we have faith in our God no matter what happens

Very few of us will ever face a test as dreadful as this one. What we learn from this lesson is that no matter what our circumstances, we do have a choice of our attitude and actions.

Finally, I would advocate that they were prepared for this situation because of their own personal relationship with God, their study of His Word and the praise and worship of they were offering Him.

They knew from their teachings as Jews that there was only ONE GOD and they would only sever, honor and worship Him. They knew how God had delivered the Jewish nation from captivity in Egypt and they would have known of His other miracles and deliverance.

It is important to note that their attitude and actions were born out of a faith in the ONE TRUE GOD! Without faith it is impossible to please God.

Paul and the Philippians

Paul is writing to the Philippians in Macedonia while he himself is in chains! He tells them to "Rejoice in the Lord always; again I will say rejoice!" Paul was the living embodiment of the right attitude. He is in Rome, in prison, in chains. Yet he pens this beautiful letter of Philippians and it is filled with joy and encouragement.

Paul uses the word JOY or REJOICING fifteen times in the book of Philippians

How is this possible? It is possible because he chooses to have a positive attitude. He does not let his circumstances dictate his actions. He will continue to exhibit the fruits of the spirit until the day he dies. I believe the verses below are an excellent example of Paul encouraging the believer to have the right attitude (and he knew that good actions would follow the proper attitude).

Philippians 4:8-9

Finally, brethren, whatever is true, whatever is honorable, whatever is right, whatever is pure, whatever is lovely, whatever is of good repute, if there is any excellence and if anything worthy of praise, dwell on these things. The things you have learned and received and heard and seen in me, practice these things, and the God of peace will be with you.

Philippians 4:4

Rejoice in the Lord always; again I will say, rejoice!

Philippians 4:11

Not that I speak from want, for I have learned to be content in whatever circumstances I am

.

Fruit of the Spirit

If you were to plant an orange tree what type of fruit would you expect it to produce? Olives? Apples? Pears?

Of course you would expect it to produce oranges. Right!   Why would you expect anything else?   An orange tree produces oranges.

When you become a Christian, what type of fruit should be evident in your life? How would you know and how would others know that you are a believer and follower of Christ.   What would your attitude and actions reveal?

What is the right attitude and actions of a Christian?   I believe that is found in Galatians 5:22-23   In these verses you will find the fruit of the sprit that should be evident in a Christians life and walk with Christ.

Attitudes – Love, Joy, Peace,

Actions – Goodness, Patience, Kindness, Faithfulness, Gentleness, Self-Control

Galatians 5:22-23

But the fruit of the Spirit is love, joy, peace, patience, kindness, goodness, faithfulness, gentleness, self-control; against such things there is no law.

This is a verse that I have memorized, taught to my children and literally have on several plaques, pictures and artwork that my bride and children have given me.   This verse so eloquently encapsulates all we are to do and be in our Christian walk.   The words are simple, but the task is difficult (because of our own selfish and sinful nature). It is only through the power of God's grace and mercy that we can even come close to living out these key attribute of the Spriit of God that dwells within us.

Love

1 Corinthians 13:4-7

Love is patient, love is kind and is not jealous; love does not brag and is not arrogant, does not act unbecomingly; it does not seek its own, is not provoked, does not take into account a wrong suffered, does not rejoice in unrighteousness, but rejoices with the truth; bears all things, believes all things, hopes all things, endures all things.

Love is one of the most powerful words in the world. No matter the language or culture, love is powerful. In 1 Corinthians chapter 13 (often referred to as the Love Chapter) we find an excellent definition of love and how it should be applied in our lives today. These words may have been written thousands of years ago, but they still resonate today as if they were freshly minted on an internet blog.
What does chapter 13 say about love?

You can have faith, speak eloquently, or be prophet, but without LOVE it is nothing!

You can give all of your possession away and even your very life, but without LOVE it is nothing.

You see, your attitude matters! You have to have the attitude of LOVE to make an actual impact in the world and to have any real meaning in live. Faith is good, Hope is good, but the greatest is LOVE.

Choose to love!

Joy

James 1:2-4

Consider it all joy, my brethren, when you encounter various trials, knowing that the testing of your faith produces endurance. And let endurance have its perfect result, so that you may be perfect and complete, lacking in nothing.

You have seen this verse several times in the book (for good reason). Joy is an attitude that we choose. It cannot be thrust upon us by someone else. You can tell if someone has joy in their life just by looking at their countenance. It is impossible to hide joy. If you are joyful, the world will know.

Peace

Philippians 4:7

And the peace of God, which surpasses all comprehension, will guard your hearts and your minds in Christ Jesus.

Unlike joy, peace is usually something that is more of an inward expression and attitude. When I think of peace I think of: Calm, Quiet, Stillness, Harmony, Tranquility and Serenity. I know when I am at peace, it is much easier for me to communicate with God and to hear from God.

Goodness

Romans 15:13-14

Now may the God of hope fill you with all joy and peace in believing, so that you will abound in hope by the power of the Holy Spirit.
And concerning you, my brethren, I myself also am convinced that you yourselves are full of goodness, filled with all knowledge and able also to admonish one another.

Goodness in the context of the believer is meeting real needs of those around us. When we are filled with Love, Joy and Peace, we will want to look for ways to meet other's needs.

Patience

Ephesians 4:2

with all humility and gentleness, with patience, showing tolerance for one another in love,

Colossians 3:12

So, as those who have been chosen of God, holy and beloved, put on a heart of compassion, kindness, humility, gentleness and patience;

How often have we jokingly said "Lord, give me patience, and give it to me right now!" While that is somewhat humorous, it is also quite true for many of us as believers today.

Patience means we are willing to trust God in His timing. Many times this means we must wait and watch – prayerfully and thoughtfully. Consider that many circumstances that are brought into your life may be there to increase your patience and build your trust in God.

Kindness

Ephesians 4:32

Be kind to one another, tender-hearted, forgiving each other, just as God in Christ also has forgiven you.

Proverbs 3:3-4

Do not let kindness and truth leave you; Bind them around your neck, Write them on the tablet of your heart. So you will find favor and good repute In the sight of God and man.

Much like goodness, kindness is an action. It is not as common these days to hear someone talk about acts of kindness, but it would be a much better world if we had more kindness.

Why is kindness so hard? Because kindness is an unselfish action and kindness does not need nor does it seek publicity or attention. Many times acts of kindness are done without the receiving party even knowing who did the act.

How do we show acts of kindness? Three way:

Word we say – a compliment to a friend or stranger, the right words in a crisis, encouraging words to one who has suffered a loss.

<u>Words we send</u> – a note, tweet, Facebook message, text, email or other form of written communication. We have some many more ways today with the incredible technology at our hands to offer kind words to someone.

<u>Things we do</u> – from simply helping a stranger change a flat tire, to picking up your neighbor's garbage can that is knocked over by the wind. There are literally and unlimited number of things we can do each day to perform acts of kindness.

However, I would suggest that kindness should start at home! Consider how you can show kindness to your spouse, children and family before you expend your energy on strangers.

Faithfulness

<u>Hebrews 10:23</u>

Let us hold fast the confession of our hope without wavering, for He who promised is faithful;

Faithfulness in this context is about the faith we have in God. One of the greatest acts of faith was when Abraham took his son Isaac to offer him as a sacrifice as God commanded. Abraham clearly loved his son (whom he and his wife had literally waited a lifetime for), but more importantly, Abraham loved and trusted God. He had the faith to follow God, even when it did not seem to make sense.

Faithfulness for us as believers today is to follow God's commands. Jesus said "If you love Me, you will keep My commandments." John 14:15

I love how Jesus kept it very simple for us to understand his commandments. He got it down to two very simple concepts in Matthew 22:36-40:

1. "'You shall love the Lord your God with all your heart, and with all your soul, and with all your mind.
2. "You shall love your neighbor as yourself."

Keep those two commandments in mind as your strive to make faithfulness a daily action and commitment to your walk with the Lord.

Gentleness

<u>Titus 3:1-2</u>

Remind them to be subject to rulers, to authorities, to be obedient, to be ready for every good deed, to malign no one, to be peaceable, gentle, showing every consideration for all men.

Gentleness and meekness are both used in this context (depending on your biblical translation). What I love about the word meekness is that it is one of the few words that Jesus used to describe his character.

Meekness does not mean weakness, it is power that is completely under control. Jesus tells us in Matthew 11:28 that he is meek/gentle and humble. If we want to have a character quality like our Lord and Savior, this is a great one to start with. However, to fully exercise this character quality, you will have to have a great abundance of self-control. Our natural tendency is to puff ourselves up and inflate both our ego and our station in life. Meekness and Humility are necessary to combat the selfishness that pervades our very thoughts and actions if we are not careful.

Self-Control

<u>2 Peter 1:5-7</u>

Now for this very reason also, applying all diligence, in your faith supply moral excellence, and in your moral excellence, knowledge, and in your knowledge, self-control, and in your self-control, perseverance, and in your perseverance, godliness, and in your godliness, brotherly kindness, and in your brotherly kindness, love.

Self-control – what does the really mean? Here are some other words that might help define self-control:

Self-Discipline
Willpower
Restraint

Self-control means being in control of your thoughts, attitude, and actions. It means controlling what can be seen by others and controlling that which can only be seen by God.

Self-control is what keeps us from spending money we don't have, to buy things we don't need, to impress people we don't know.

Self-control is about putting filters on what we allow into or mind through our eyes or ears.

Self-control is about regulating what we consume on a daily basis and not giving into gluttony and self-indulgence.

Self-control is about being thoughtful of the words that will proceed from our mouth, pen, keyboard, computer, phone, tablet or any other electronic device that will ever be invented. Most of the time this means writing a draft that NEVER gets sent.

Self-control is about having a time of study, pray, praise and worship. It is being thoughtful on how you will spend your time, talents and treasures.

Self-control is impossible in and of ourselves. It is only through the saving grace and mercy of Jesus and the Holy Spirt living inside us that allows us to have godly self-control.

When you consider all of the fruits of the spirit, it is self-control that allows us to be used by God in such a way that will bring honor and glory to Him and His kingdom.

As you consider your actions and attitudes and know that these are the two things that you can control in the middle of the crisis, make a commitment to memorize Galatians 5:22-23. Imprint this verse on your heart, mind, body and soul. Make it a part of who you are and believe and know that victorious Christian living comes when we fully live out the fruits of the sprit.

Quotes on Attitude

"Life is 10% what happens to me and 90% of how I react to it." – Charles Swindoll

"People may hear your words, but they feel your attitude. John C. Maxwell

"Attitude is a little thing that makes a big difference." Winston Churchill

"We cannot change our past. We cannot change the fact that people act in a certain way. We ca not change the inevitable. The only thing we can do is play on the one string we have, and that is our attitude." Charles R. Swindoll

"I am still determined to be cheerful and happy, in whatever situation I may be; for I have also learned from experience that the greater part of our happiness or misery depends upon our dispositions, and not upon our circumstances." Martha Washington

"Oh, my friend, it's not what they take away from you that counts. It's what you do with what you have left." Hubert Humphrey

"No life is so hard that you can't make it easier by the way you take it". Ellen Glasgow

"We cannot direct the wind but we can adjust the sails." Author Unknown

"Every day may not be good, but there's something good in every day" Author Unknown

"Nothing can stop the man with the right mental attitude from achieving his goal; nothing on earth can help the man with the wrong mental attitude." Thomas Jefferson

Quotes on Actions

"Do you want to know who you are? Don't ask. Act! Action will delineate and define you." Thomas Jefferson

"Action is the foundational key to all success." Pablo Picasso

"Small deeds done are better than great deeds planned."
 Peter Marshall

"You don't have to be great to start, but you have to start to be great."
Zig Ziglar

"An ant on the move does more than a dozing ox." ~ Lao Tzu

"Things may come to those who wait, but only the things left by those who hustle." ~ Abraham Lincoln

"The superior man is modest in his speech but exceeds in his actions."
Confucius

"God provides the wind, but man must raise the sails."
St. Augustine

"Never confuse motion with action."
Benjamin Franklin

"I never worry about action, but only inaction."
Winston Churchill

"Weakness of attitude becomes weakness of character. "
Albert Einstein

Scripture to Memorize

James 1:2-4

Consider it all joy, my brethren, when you encounter various trials, knowing that the testing of your faith produces endurance. And let endurance have its perfect result, so that you may be perfect and complete, lacking in nothing.

Jeremiah 29:11-13

For I know the plans that I have for you,' declares the Lord, 'plans for welfare and not for calamity to give you a future and a hope. Then you will call upon Me and come and pray to Me, and I will listen to you. You will seek Me and find Me when you search for Me with all your heart.

John 16:33

These things I have spoken to you, so that in Me you may have peace. In the world you have tribulation, but take courage; I have overcome the world."

Philippians 4:6-7

Be anxious for nothing, but in everything by prayer and supplication with thanksgiving let your requests be made known to God. And the peace of God, which surpasses all comprehension, will guard your hearts and your minds in Christ Jesus.

Philippians 4:13

I can do all things through Him who strengthens me.

1 Peter 5:7

casting all your anxiety on Him, because He cares for you.

Isaiah 41:10

'Do not fear, for I am with you;
Do not anxiously look about you, for I am your God.
I will strengthen you, surely I will help you,
Surely I will uphold you with My righteous right hand.'

Psalm 9:9-10

The Lord also will be a stronghold for the oppressed,
A stronghold in times of trouble;
And those who know Your name will put their trust in You,
For You, O Lord, have not forsaken those who seek You.

Romans 8:18

For I consider that the sufferings of this present time are not worthy to be compared with the glory that is to be revealed to us.

1 Peter 1:6-7

In this you greatly rejoice, even though now for a little while, if necessary, you have been distressed by various trials, so that the proof of your faith, being more precious than gold which is perishable, even though tested by fire, may be found to result in praise and glory and honor at the revelation of Jesus Christ;

Joshua 1:9

Have I not commanded you? Be strong and courageous! Do not tremble or be dismayed, for the Lord your God is with you wherever you go."

Jesus as the example

Jesus

As we think about the three things we should continue to do when we have Trials, Trouble or Tribulation, we do not have to look any further than the example that Jesus sets for all us.   Here we will see Jesus in a situation where he will apply all three of these at one time.

> **Jesus will pray**
> **Jesus will participate in fellowship**
> **Jesus will praise and worship**

In Matthew 26, we find the story of Jesus praying in the garden of Gethsemane. Jesus has just finished the last supper with all of his disciples and it was his last opportunity to pour into them and fellowship with them before his trial and crucifixion.   Jesus knows the physical pain that is coming and the ultimate separation from the Father as he dies for the sins of the world.   So where do his thoughts turn?   They turn to prayer.

Jesus was clearly distressed as he knew what was coming.   In verse 37-38 the bible says he was "grieved and distressed".   He went deeper into the garden and took his three closest disciple with him (Peter, James and John) and asked them to stay with him while he prayed.   He even said this to them: "My soul is deeply grieved, to the point of death; remain here and keep watch with Me."

You see even our Lord and Savior knew that in time of trouble, the first thing to do was to pray to the Father. In addition, we also see that in this time of distress Jesus wanted to keep close fellowship with his disciples not only to continue to teach them, but also to have them as prayer partners and to help encourage Him.

Finally we see in Jesus's prayer that he shows the **highest form of worship** to God our Father. He asks for the "cup" to pass from him, but then he say "not my will, but your will be done". God is looking for all of us to be obedient to His call in our life. Here Jesus knows what is coming and yet surrenders his own will to that of the Father. You see, obedience is the highest form of worship we can give back to God.

It is a great example of us to know that in our times of trouble we should first turn to the Father in prayer and lift our voice to Him and continue in fellowship with other believers so that we will be encouraged and can even encourage others. Finally we know we can and should praise and worship God no matter the circumstances in our life.

The Garden of Gethsemane

Matthew 26:36-46

Then Jesus came with them to a place called Gethsemane, and said to His disciples, "Sit here while I go over there and pray."

And He took with Him Peter and the two sons of Zebedee, and began to be grieved and distressed. Then He said to them, "My soul is deeply grieved, to the point of death; remain here and keep watch with Me."

And He went a little beyond them, and fell on His face and prayed, saying, "My Father, if it is possible, let this cup pass from Me; yet not as I will, but as You will."

And He came to the disciples and found them sleeping, and said to Peter, "So, you men could not keep watch with Me for one hour? Keep watching and praying that you may not enter into temptation; the spirit is willing, but the flesh is weak."

He went away again a second time and prayed, saying, "My Father, if this cannot pass away unless I drink it, Your will be done."

Again He came and found them sleeping, for their eyes were heavy. And He left them again, and went away and prayed a third time, saying the same thing once more.

Then He came to the disciples and said to them, "Are you still sleeping and resting? Behold, the hour is at hand and the Son of Man is being betrayed into the hands of sinners. Get up, let us be going; behold, the one who betrays Me is at hand!"

Finally, consider Jesus attitude and actions as he faces this situation. His attitude is one of love for the world and for His creation. His actions are those of obedience to the Father. He does not pray one time in this scene, he prays three times to the Father. Jesus is and continues to be the perfect model for our lives and how we should ultimately face the trials, trouble and tribulations that **WILL** come in our lifetime.

Summary

As I completed this book, it dawned on me that I have covered an incredible amount of material. It has taken me over 8 months to research, pray and compose this book and if for nothing other than my own edification, I thought it would be a good idea to create a summary that pulls all of the key points together at the end of the book.

Storms - Trials Troubles and Tribulation

✓ Jesus tells us that we will have tribulation in this world, but that he has overcome the world

✓ Paul tells us that the tribulations will come, but that they are there to develop Godly character in our lives

✓ James tells us that we should consider it all joy as the trials test our faith to further refine us

✓ Paul tells us that we should comfort and encourage others who are going through trials that we have already been through.

✓ God will be with us

Prayer Recap

There were three key themes from this chapter that we learned:

- ✓ Why Pray – because it is effective and God is listening

- ✓ When should we pray – all the time!

- ✓ What should our posture be when we pray? It does not matter! God can hear your prayers no matter the position of you body.

Participate in Fellowship Recap

We learned two main things in this chapter

- ✓ We all need encouragement in times of trials, trouble and tribulation (and we cannot encourage ourselves).

- ✓ We can encourage others who will be traveling down the same path that that we have already trodden.

Praise & Worship Recap

So what have we learned about praise and worship in times of trials, troubles and tribulation?

- ✓ Praise and Worship is a choice we make

- ✓

Praise & Worship Recap

✓ We can choose to praise God based on His character even when we do not feel like praising Him.

✓ <u>Who</u> should praise God? Everyone and Everything

✓ <u>What</u> is praise?   Praise is an outward expression of the inner faith we have in God.

✓ <u>Where</u> should we praise God? Everywhere

✓ <u>When</u> should we praise God? All the time

✓ <u>Why</u> should we praise God? Because He is worthy of praise

✓ <u>How</u> should we praise God? With our heart, mind, body and soul

Actions and Attitude

✓ It is our choice and we can choose to control our attitude and actions.

✓ The fruits of the sprit should guide our attitude and actions

Attitudes – Love, Joy, Peace,

Actions – Goodness, Patience, Kindness, Faithfulness, Gentleness, Self-Control

Finally

Jesus is our perfect example.

Notes

Notes

Final Thoughts

First, thank you so much for taking the time to read this book. It is my prayer that this has been a blessing to you and your family.

Secondly, if you have an opportunity to send me an e-mail with your thoughts, comments or suggestions, that would be very helpful.

Finally, I hope you were encouraged and strengthened by what you read.

paulbeersdorf@gmail.com

Blessings to you and your family!

Paul Beersdorf